FORD COBRA

GUIDE

By
BILL CARROLL

MODERN SPORTS CAR SERIES

TAB BOOKS
Blue Ridge Summit, Pa. 17214

FIRST EDITION

NOVEMBER 1977

Copyright © 1964 by TAB BOOKS

Printed in the United States
of America

Reproduction or publication of the content in any manner, without express permission of the publisher, is prohibited. No liability is assumed with respect to the use of the information herein.

Hardbond Edition: International Standard Book No. 0-8306-9991-0

Paperbound Edition: International Standard Book No. 0-8306-2007-9

Library of Congress Card Number: 64-18159

DEDICATION

With grateful appreciation for the valued efforts of Douglas Armstrong, one of England's finest motoring journalists.

Contents

		Page
1.	**Shel's Story**	
	Carroll Shelby reveals the short exciting history of his Ford-Cobra	5
2.	**A.C. Cars, the Specialist Builders**	
	Behind Cobra production is one of England's finest sports car builders	29
3.	**Production—a Climb for Quality**	
	How the Cobras are built in America, to custom quality ..	48
4.	**Production Cobras on the Street**	
	Ken Miles presents his approach to enjoying a Cobra....	67
5.	**Building Racing Cobras**	
	Behind the scenes story of Shelby American technique to build a race-winning sports car	79
6.	**Engine Modification to Win**	
	Cecil Bowman, master tuner, details his work with super-powered Ford V8 engines	96
7.	**Ken Miles on Competition Cobras**	
	Ken explains his driving methods and passes along a wealth of ideas	123

"I build the Cobra with my heart, rather than . . . for a profit."
—Carroll Shelby, 1964.

1. Shel's Story

I think the only real interests I've ever had in my life are flying and race cars. When I was only 7 or 8 years old my dad took me to all the bull-ring circuits he could find around Dallas.

During the war I was a pilot in the Training Command where I flew just about everything they had. Twin-engine Beeches, the 25s, the 26s, the old B-18s (a "mother" version of the DC-3) and finally the B-29—just before I got out in 1945.

There were a couple of close calls. Once, a clock blew out of the instrument panel and broke my nose, and once I had to bail out over the Matador Range in West Texas. That time I walked all night to find help. Had I taken a different fork in the road I'd have walked one mile into the town of Matador. As it was I took the wrong fork and walked 35 miles clear across the second largest ranch in the world!

After the war I tried several businesses but finally decided to do what I had always wanted—drive race cars. I got into the sports car game and drove for about a year as an amateur. My first winner was an old MG-TC, and the next a Jaguar XK120. Then I picked up an Allard. I drove that for about ten races which gave me enough experience to leave Texas and go down and race in Argentina. There I only finished tenth but John Fitch, who was with Aston Martin, offered to take me to Europe. I went over for about a year and when I came back went to California for John Edgar and in 1957 won the National SCCA Championship with a Ferrari.

In 1958 I was again driving for Aston Martin in Europe who, in '58 and '59, won the world's championship. Then back to the States as a national sports car driving champ in 1960. I retired that year to California when my doctor told me that my heart wouldn't stand that kind of the excitement

At that time I became seriously interested in producing a personal car. In 1957, I had talked about this with Dick Hall. We decided to go into business, in Dallas, with a sports car agency. Our idea was to someday turn out a sports car with an American engine and a chassis built in Europe or Japan.

About the same time I was talking with General Motors' Ed Cole who was vice president and general manager of Chevrolet. He seemed to be pretty much for it and talked to Harvey Earl who at the time was in charge of styling at General Motors. They were very encouraging but the people in charge of the Corvette program found a number of obstacles to my project. I kept looking for a different way to do it and even talked with various manufacturers while racing in Europe. My real point in driving in European competition wasn't because I loved it. It was because I was trying to find out how limited-production manufacturers, such as Aston Martin, Ferrari and Maserati, put things together, made them work and made a profit. Two or three times during my racing period I was on the verge of building my prototype of a sports car, and when I retired I made up my mind I was going to do it. I was able to get the distributorship of Goodyear racing tires which helped me get started. For that I'll always be thankful to Goodyear. Believe me, its not always easy for an ex racing driver to get started in business.

About that time the Bristol Aeroplane Company quit manufacturing A.C. Cars Ltd.'s automobile engines. That left A.C. with a fairly good chassis and no engine, I was sitting in the office with Dean Moon, who knew I was going to build my car. He mentioned that Ford had a dandy little engine of 221 cubic inches and my project sounded like something they could be interested in. I picked up the telephone and called Dave Evans in Dearborn, in Ford's performance evaluation section.

I told Dave about my project and asked if he thought Ford would be interested. In a couple of days he called back and asked if I could go to Dearborn—which I did. We discussed my ideas with Don Frey, at that time engineering manager in charge of development. Don and Dave were so interested they decided to lend me a couple of their new engines.

I had already contacted A.C. to ask if they were interested. They said 'Yes', so in October, 1962 I took a trip to Europe and talked with them. We started building a prototype in the A.C. Cars Ltd. shop in England. We took an ordinary A.C. that had previously been using the Bristol engine and began to modify it. A.C. had been building this car for years and they knew how to get things done. They had their own engineering department which redesigned the rear end because we knew that the rear axle and shaft stubs wouldn't take the horsepower of the Ford V-8 engine. That's one thing about a small compact company—they can make changes very quickly—and we had no trouble.

We dropped the 221-cubic-inch engine in, tested it, and it seemed to work all right with this version of the Fairlane V-8. But when we got over to the MIRA test track, which belongs to the Association of Motor Manufacturers, we found out a lot of things needed fixing. Front spindles and bearings weren't large enough so we had to redesign them. Parts of the chassis had to be strengthened and the front spring lengthened. A-frames were changed and the A-arms modified. From the time we started building the prototype until it was finished in February of 1962, took about three months. Only two people drove this—Derek Hurlock, one of the directors of A.C. Car Ltd., and myself.

I was given fabulous cooperation by A.C. They were producing one hundred cars a year and suddenly we started talking about five hundred. Traditionally they are in the

Shortly after its introduction, in 1953, the Ace was in competition. Derek Hurlock (son of Charles F. Hurlock) a director of the company; put the Ace through its paces in a "Club Meeting" at Silverstone, on Saturday, May 29, 1954. At this time the Ace was powered by the single overhead camshaft version of the A.C. "Light Six" engine which had been in production since 1922.

business of building wheel chairs and invalid carriages for the British Government. The automobile end of the business, a kind of sideline, is the love of William Hurlock, the managing director. He and his brother Charles like anything on wheels—to the point where they built locomotives for the British Government during the last war!

The 221-cubic-inch Fairlane V-8 engines that we had over in England for mock-up and testing purposes we left there, and when the first prototype arrived we found that the 260 high-performance Fairlane V-8 engine was available from Ford. It was a pretty plain engine with a four barrel carburetor, a hot cam and solid lifters.

Bill Carroll Comments

Behind Carroll Shelby's simple description of modifications to the first prototype lies an interesting story. At the time it arrived in California, Carroll Shelby was operating from a little shop in Santa Fe Springs with accessory manufacturer Dean Moon. Here he had the distributorship for Goodyear racing tires and at Riverside International Raceway ran a driving school.

When the first A.C. arrived, by air freight, there was no

way to get it to the shop in Santa Fe Springs. One of the fellows being trained at the Shelby driving school had a trailer for his Ferrari. This was borrowed, hooked to a pickup truck, and a crew of Moon's people sent to the airport to pick up the new car. It was unpainted and had huge stickers all over, indicating that it was "for export only," there was no water in the engine, and oil should be added before it was driven! Inside the car was completely trimmed. Under the hood was—nothing. This was CSX-0001, which stands for Carroll Shelby Experimental.

The first powerplant installed in CSX0001 was an early Ford 260. All of Dean Moon's staff pitched in when the car arrived to make the engine installation. Eight hours after the A.C. was unloaded, it was operable, the unpainted aluminum body polished to silver brilliance. Later a number of wild camshaft configurations, different carburetor setups and ignition changes were tried in Dean Moon's accessory plant. Luckily there was so much room in the A.C. engine compartment that weight balance turned out exactly right.

That this first car was something less than perfect can be deduced from observations of Pete Brock, Carroll Shelby's early test driver. As Pete puts it, "I had been racing a Lotus that season. Handling differences between the Lotus and that first Cobra were really something. In a Lotus you go around the corner and you don't move your hand more than three inches to make the corner. In the driving position you sit relaxed, back in the car, and very low to the ground. The Lotus seldom broke away and if it did it was subtle.

"Compare that with sitting way up high on top of two frame rails, herding a V-8 engine that's bellowing, screaming and leaning, while everything seems to be bucking loose in it. I knew the Cobra was going fast but it didn't exactly impress me as being an up-to-date car. It seemed to be getting the job done in spite of itself. Yet everytime I went out in it for testing, my desire to drive it in competition built up to the point where I really 'hurt' to drive the Cobra in a race."

Shelby explains his selection of the name thus: "When I

woke up one night in 1956 and decided I was going to build a car some way, no matter how long it took, I got to thinking about a name. The name Cobra came to me—I can't explain why. It just seemed like an aesthetic name from an aesthetic animal. All through the years of trying to put this thing together, I never changed my mind and never doubted that I would call my car 'The Cobra.'

"I ran into resistance to the name every once in a while when I talked to various companies, but I was adamant that 'Cobra' was what the car should be called. As far as legal aspects of the name go, there was another company, Crosley, which called their little engine Cobra (for COpper BRAzed), but Crosley has since gone out of business."

Because Carroll Shelby realized that racing was where he would make his name, the first chassis was given a workout at Riverside Raceway. Mechanics knew they could spend 15,000 miles on a proving ground, under controlled conditions, and not learn as much as they would find in a single race. Sports car driver Billy Krause started the testing with Pete Brock as alternate. Engine tuner Bill Likes was setting up engines with Ole Olson as his assistant. Early tests on the Riverside track showed a number of things that needed correction. Carburetion was a problem because the Ford V-8 engine was running a stock four-barrel carburetor. At high speeds on corners the float bowl would allow the carburetor to dry or flood causing loss of control in the turns. One of the early modifications was the installation of a Holly carburetor. Because there were no anti-roll bars on the car the chassis would lean a great deal which made the carburetor problem even worse so anti-roll bars were installed at front and rear of the chassis. Special exhaust headers were added similar to those used on the V-8 engines run by Lance Reventlow.

Shel Goes On:

We continued testing at Riverside and testing on the street. Then we took it back to Ford in Dearborn. We could do things quickly, from an engineering standpoint, and build something in a hurry. But when you have to analyze your problems, a large company can come to your rescue and save months and even years of work.

At Ford we started working. One thing we had was a heating problem. We found we weren't getting air out of the engine compartment and the radiator, as far as we were concerned, was too small. Airflow wasn't adequate. Our grille was the wrong shape. Impellers had to be cut down on the water pumps, as we were pumping too much water through the V-8 engine. We also found that our header tank was too low. Actually the biggest problem we ever had with the Cobra was cooling because of our very small air inlet in the nose of the body. For a while we talked about an aluminum radiator and then decided it wasn't worth the weight saving. Life of a standard radiator is so much longer, and cooling quality is so much better. Consequently, we ran about 10 degrees cooler with a copper and brass radiator Ford got McCord Radiator Co. to design for us. We can honestly say that instruments, wiring harness, radiator, type of electrical systems, including headlights, tail lights and turn indicators, came directly from Ford's engineering re-evaluation program. This was all done before we decided to go ahead and build Cobras in batches of 500.

The original idea had been to build only a couple hundred Cobras. You have to build one hundred to enter the SCCA production class. Because Ford was interested enough to go along, A.C. was willing to help build the first hundred bodies. So I put $40,000—all I could scrape up—in prototype cost, engineering and development of the first car. Between that, A.C. and Ford we were able to put the first hundred cars together.

Don Frey and Ray Geddes arranged for me to market the car through Ford dealers in the United States. We felt we'd be able to sell our hundred cars to a hundred dealers who would buy one for themselves!

One thing about racing is—there's no secrets. When the

word got around, we soon had enough Ford dealers interested to know we could sell 200. Before we finished the first hundred we gave A.C. a contract for the second. We decided to have the first hundred bodies and chassis built complete in England and decided on the A.C. aluminum body.

As Bill Carroll Saw It:

Carroll was in Dearborn worrying about selling a hundred cars, his first orders actually came from people knocking at the door of his small shop in Santa Fe Springs saying, "Is this where Shelby is building his car?"

There were young fellows interested in racing who wanted early cars because they realized they might clean up. One man who bought one of the early cars drives it as sharp as the day it rolled out of the shop. Early buyers had to leave a thousand dollar deposit for their cars. Delivery took about sixty days. Some buyers would come down every day to watch each screw put into their special car.

Price of these early cars was $5995, the target price to which the Shelby organization has held. Everyone thought that price would go up but Shelby American has made certain it has remained stable. The Cobra team racer costs slightly over $9,000—the original price established for that car. A less expensive, $6150, racer was announced in 1964.

In October of 1962, race-ready Cobra CSX0002 made its first appearance at the Riverside Raceway in California. The car had a mildly tuned version of the 260-cubic-inch V-8 running a single four-barrel carburetor. Billy Krause was driving. Though the Cobra was beautifully prepared, it created no real commotion with spectators who saw it as just another car.

A LeMans start had cars lined up on Riverside's back straightaway underneath the bridge. It was a terrific start with drivers running across the track, hopping into their cars and booming off. Dave McDonald, who now drives for Shelby American, was at that time driving a white Corvette coupe. He made a terrific start and was at least half the length of the straightaway ahead of everybody in the first lap. The Cobra caught up within a couple of laps and then proceeded to walk on and leave McDonald sitting. A few laps further the Cobra, coming around Turn 9, spun out when overstressed metal of the left rear hub snapped. One lonely Cobra came limping into the pit. It was the end of Shelby's race but the car had shown spectators what it was capable of. By the time it was a static display in the pit area, it was surrounded by eager questioners. Within four days Shelby American engineer Phil Remington had a new hub design, forgings were made, and the car was race ready again.

Shel's Early Production Efforts

Everything was constant change. I couldn't say whether the first ten or the first 35 were the same. We found that people's feet got so hot that we had to put in a ventilation system. We hadn't made much provision for a heater in the first bunch because we didn't realize we had a street car that was so desirable. When people who bought them in the northern states began complaining, we had to put a heater on.

At first we sold them all with Goodyear racing tires and as most everybody knows a racing tire is certainly no good for the street. There really wasn't a good tire available at that time. I think we've all got better sports car tires now because Goodyear built a tire for my car. Similar tires are now original equipment for Lincolns and Thunderbirds. Competitive tire companies are copying our tire design with standard equipment on competitive automobiles. It's a premium tire that would fit any car. Engineers call it a high efficiency tire.

Then we made some changes to the interior and changed the paint. I never cease to be amazed at Cobra buyers. We started out building just red and white cars. There were a lot of complaints, customers wanted other colors. So we went to black, blue, maroon and green. Now we sell more red and white cars than any other color.

We started the first hundred cars in December, 1962. It took us three or four months to turn them out. I'm not sure of the number we built in Santa Fe Springs, but there must have been between twenty or thirty. We built them one at a time. Capacity was about two a week. When we moved to Venice (where the factory is now located) we could work on five at a time and production rose to about five cars a week soon after we arrived. This was a lot better than the operation at Santa Fe Springs where we had extra chassis and bodies stored in the open under tarpaulins. There was a little shed for the engines which we kept locked up until we needed them.

We built approximately 75 Cobras with the 260-cubic-inch V-8 engine. When the 289 came out we switched over to that. Every once in a while some customer brings back a 260 and we change it for a 289 which gives just about what you would expect. There is about a 25 or 30 horsepower difference.

Initial Improvements

One factor that decided the organization's move to Venice was that it would be close to Los Angeles International Airport. As the racing business relies heavily on free movement between nations, air transportation is important. Thus Shelby American, in Venice, California, is only 24 hours away from the parts warehouse of A.C. Cars Ltd. in England.

In a matter of months, after arriving in the new expanded quarters, Shelby American employed over 35 people including racing mechanics. The early production cars were arriving in a steady flow with small shipments each week. At that time extra work was necessary to make necessary modifications while building the car. Motor mounts and radiator brackets must be put in the right location and new clutch tubing be properly installed. None of these changes are necessary on current production Corbras, as all modifications have been completed at the factory in England. Cobras now arrive ready for cleaning and building into a completed sports roadster.

It's worth noting that while Shelby American mechanics were preparing their cars to run at Daytona, in early 1963, the Ford Motor Company also had them testing new engines with an aluminum block. These same engines were used most successfully at Indianapolis later in 1963. Ford engineers asked Shelby to help because they were concerned with oil consumption. They were testing extremely loose clearances on running components to reduce internal friction. They needed an overall picture of oil consumption, and wanted to know if other problems would crop up under high speed running circumstances they had not experienced in dynomometer testing.

Ford had no trouble with oil consumption or oil clearances, but they did have a most unusual problem with Welch plugs used to seal casting holes in the block. In most engines, Welch plugs are pressed into casting holes where they remain because the steel Welch plug contracts and expands at about the same rate as does the cast iron engine block. However, these experimental blocks of aluminum were using a steel plug. The aluminum block, when it got hot, would expand faster than the steel plug and allow the plug to loosen. Water pressure of the cooling system at high speed blew the Welch plug out of one engine an hour and a half before a race. Shelby American mechanics, in the ninety minutes alloted, had to replace an engine and send Dan Gurney out on the track a half lap after the race had started. As a result, Ford put screwed plugs in all casting holes of their aluminum blocks.

After the Daytona race, which ended disasterously when a chankshaft damper broke and jammed the steering, the Shelby American team regrouped its forces and began preparing cars for Sebring. They had two new cars which arrived from England with the rack and pinion steering system. Initial testing of the rack and pinion cars was done by Ken Miles. When cars arrived, Shelby American mechanics dropped a ready engine into one of the chassis and sent Ken to Riverside to do testing. Improvements in the rack and pinion car were so great that he was able to cut two seconds off lap time as compared to the conventional worm and sector car. The Cobra steered so much better at the front, and held so well, that it was necessary to go to a smaller size tire in the rear to make the back wheels stick.

Drivers first noticed improvement in rack and pinion steering over worm and sector in making an "S" corner. With the worm and sector car there is weight transference as the car leans from entry to exit of the "S" in a fast sweeping line. Normally, Cobra drivers had to go slightly to the left and then slightly to the right, to maintain control. As the Cobra went from left to right, with worm and sector steering, there was a neutral position in steering in which the car would tend to wander and the driver had to keep adjusting the steering. Not only was this difficult but the worm and sector was extremely stiff. When driving a rack and pinion car the drivers are able to go through the S's with only the slightest twist of the steering wheel and no mid-turn sensation of wandering.

Caroll Shelby's efforts at Sebring in 1963 were probably more education than racing. Just about everything that could go wrong went wrong during the race. Everything on the cars that could be rattled off was found later on the track. Four attachment bolts sheared off the steering rack and pinion assembly because the bolts were of hardware, rather than aircraft, quality.

Brakes came in for their share of attention and adequate brake cooling proved a must. At Sebring there are many sharp corners, one of which slows the car down to almost 10 miles an hour. After a few minutes of racing, brakes reach and hold such high heat that cooling is a paramount problem for success in the event. Phil Hill's car at Sebring ran over a road marker which struck the caliper assembly on a front wheel. This knocked the cooling scoop against the disc so that it covered more of the disc than would normally have been protected. Reduced air flow across the disc caused the brake to heat severely. Brakes were being used so frequently that pads on this wheel burned completely through the lining and steel backing. When the car finally came into the pit, Phil Hill had been using the brake piston to stop the car. Mechanics had to pry the entire caliper apart to repair it.

Another thing learned at Sebring was that the oil pump could give trouble under competition stresses. Vibration and

CSX 0002, with Billy Krause driving, bends a sweeping left at Riverside International Raceway. This was the first showing of Cobra in October 1962, as a race car.

hammering from the track rattled the pickup tube off the pump casting. This tube extends downward from the oil pump intake into the sump of the crankcase. As the pump could no longer draw oil from the sump, the engine would dry and eventually suffer bearing failure. In Cobra racing engines the pickup tube has been reinforced and a special bracket built to eliminate vibration problems with the pump gear housing. Ford production engines have been modified so there is no chance of failure in either of these parts during normal use of the Cobra engine.

Special transmission gear ratios made for Sebring proved to be desirable. Accordingly, in early 1964, they were made into an optional gear set available to all Cobra purchasers.

One of the modifications made to the 289-cubic-inch Ford engines to get greater horsepower was installation of side-draft Weber carburetors. Phil Remington, chief engineer for Shelby American, designed a set of ram-tube-mounted Webers which added something like 75 horsepower to the engine. At that time down-draft Webers were not available. Unfortunately, the Weber side-draft manifold was so bulky that it proved impractical as a performance option. Eventually the first down-draft Webers arrived.

The first car which Carroll Shelby built in Santa Fe Springs was used primarily as a demonstrator and to check out production requirements. One of the complaints about Cobras was inadequate weather protection in northern parts of the United States. This is understandable because the first car was built and driven in Southern California where weather protection is a minimum requirement.

An amusing situation involving this first car was that no one could figure how to put the top up. Though advertised by A.C. as a "one-man" top, there were no instructions with the car. The problem was not getting the top out of the well but in fitting the leading edge of the fabric to the upper frame of the windshield in such a way that it would remain in place when the car was driven at speed. Eventually, Shelby found an Ace owner in Southern California who had the same top

Wheel mounted closer to instrument panel, where instruments have been modified and relocated for clarity and ease of reading.

on his car and taught them how to put the top on the first Cobra.

Unfortunately, this first car was never really run hard enough to find the problems which occured when later Cobras were put onto the race track. It already had modifications to the rear suspension and differential stub shafts but improvements in handling and steering would certainly have been made on the original production cars had it been possible to enter Carroll Shelby's CSX0001 in serious competition. This car was licensed in California as an A.C. Cobra and driven everywhere by everyone. Carroll used it for personal transportation and it was one of the early vehicles tested by many magazine writers in Southern California.

There were no bumper guards available for the Cobra at that time and frequently it would suffer front or rear end dam-

19

age. Though interested drivers usually took extremely good care of the car, about 25 percent of the time it was returned to Shelby with dents in the body. Many of these resulted from people leaning or sitting on the fenders. The welded seams were so soft dents would form in the aluminum at little more than a glance.

As Shelby Tells It

There wasn't any really serious problem with the steering. It didn't make any difference on the street but worm and sector steering in competition changed radically as the front end of the car moved up and down. We only built 125 cars with worm and sector steering before changing over to the rack and pinion system we now use.

Nevertheless, reporters thought our car was great. They considered it extremely well designed, and believed there was a definite market for it. We all had felt for years that building an American-English sports car should have been done sooner. Americans like to have plenty of torque which just makes sense. We've been used to torque in our engines. This Ford engine is an improvement that made an extremely pliable car which drove very well on the street. The Cobra had a lot of acceleration, in fact more acceleration than probably any production car ever had until that time. This seemed to be just what the press thought a sports car should be.

We've done a lot of re-evaluation since the first Cobra. It wasn't long before we found that we had the wrong rear axle ratio—3.54 to 1—which we had put under the first 125 cars. We decided to change this to a 3.77 to give the Cobra a little more acceleration away from stop signs. A driver can go 140 miles an hour with a 3.77 and it's very seldom he'll go much faster than that.

Then we put the ventilation system in, with inlet ducts on the front of the car. As far as the street version is concerned, one of the things I insisted we do was go to a wider rim so that a buyer could race the car on the same rims that he uses on the street. All we needed was a new tire which Goodyear agreed to build for us. About this time we realized that for competition we'd have to have a larger oil pan. Possibly it would be good for street use under a harder driver. Now we're incorporating into our performance version, and making available as an option, an oversize cast aluminum oil pan.

Now that we have built over 400 cars (as of January, 1964) a lot of things that we discussed in our re-evaluation are coming to pass. A constant state of development, in our racing engine department, has been going on for a year and a half. The first thing we really improved of Ford's outside of adding Weber carburetors, were our Sebring engines of 1963. We were pulling 330 to 335 horsepower out of the 289-cubic-inch V-8. We did this by adding larger valves, cleaning up ports and balancing the engines piece by piece. In putting them together, we set up a little more tolerance than their production high-performance engines. You see we can get the pistons set to any tolerance we want, the main bearings, and so forth. This is one thing that's come out of our development work with the Cobra.

Ford is now building these engines for me. They come off of the engine assembly line at Ford's Cleveland plant and we install them in the Cobra making no changes except to replace the plain steel valve covers with Cobra valve covers. This is the very same engine that's in the Fairlane 289 high-performance models. We offer some options, such as dual four-barrel carburetors and so forth, which are sold through Ford dealers as the Cobra Kit. Other than that, these are standard engines that Ford puts in a box and mails to us here at Shelby American.

A.C. Cars puts on all the brackets for the engine mounts, radiator brackets and transmission hangers. Everything we add to the car bolts right onto brackets already installed. Anything built in England is about a third of the cost here. We build what we can overseas because of savings in using European labor. Before putting an engine in we clean the chassis and check on all the assembly bolts. We straighten everything and touch up before dropping the engine in from the top.

Early Arrivals and Changes Made

As mentioned earlier, Carroll's personal prototype car was the first Cobra. The second, modified into a race machine, began its eventful career at Riverside Raceway in October, 1962. The next cars, three in number, arrived as a group. They had to be hastily prepared, assembled and repainted for an exhibit in Dearborn. On arrival it was discovered the shades of paint weren't right. Shelby American painters had been working under fluorescent lights; in Dearborn the Cobras were to be shown under incandescent. They had to be completely repainted before they could be displayed. At this writing all three cars were in the Dearborn area. Henry Ford II is said to have one he enjoys as personal transportation. A second car was sent to the styling department and a special hardtop body made for it. The third was stripped of its Cobra body and the chassis used as the frame for a custom body built by the Ford Styling Division—the Cougar II.

In mid-1963 many of the race-developed Cobra modifications became available to Ford buyers as part of the Cobra Kits. Among the first were aluminum valve covers. Then Shelby announced an aluminum manifold which would handle the large 390 V-8 four-barrel carburetor. A special manifold for racing, which would hold the four 481BM Weber downdrafts, was made available to racing Cobra owners. They also could purchase various Shelby American manifold and exhaust systems to improve performance of their engine. Steel scatter shields, designed after Shelby's experience at Daytona Beach, and the cast steel clutch housing, soon became Cobra Kit options.

Many items of the Cobra Kit are modifications of high-performance parts from Ford V-8 engines. For instance the 289 two-barrel engine and certain models of the 260 can use Cobra Kit parts. There is even a manifold which will accept three two-barrel Holly carburetors. The cast-aluminum crankcase sump, which increases ability of oil to cool the engine, has a capacity of about 6-½ quarts. If it were to fit only one model it could be much larger. Unfortunately Ford cars using the 289 V-8 engine have their steering linkage in different positions. Accordingly, cross members more or less dictate the size of the sump. Shelby American engineers couldn't design any one sump to fit all three cars.

Exhaust headers are available to Ford owners to improve performance of any Fairlane model. The 289 V-8 high performance exhaust headers are much more efficient than headers used on the standard 289 or 260-cubic-inch V-8s. These are cast exhaust manifolds, a production item from Ford. Even more efficient are fabricated tube headers produced by Derrington in England. The original design for these fabricated headers was by Shelby American. In pricing them for production it was found that they could be manufactured in England at less cost. They are made for both the Shelby Cobra racing cars as well as an optional extra for all Ford 289-powered passenger cars.

Another performance item available from Shelby American is a dual point distributor with more desirable spark curve. It is more durable than the single point, production distributor and does not have a vacuum advance, A straight mechanical advance is more suitable for maximum performance from the 289 four-barrel engines. In addition a number of dress-up items, common to the Falcon Sprint, are available to Cobra and Fairlane owners. These are plated covers, plated air cleaner, plated radiator cap and chrome hydraulic fluid reservoir caps.

For the Fairlane owner interested in maximum performance a cylinder head kit is available. It is made from production heads used on the 289-cubic-inch V-8. These heads will fit on any 289 and the 260 Fairlane engines. They have larger valves, higher compression ratio, machined retainer areas for heavier valve springs and screwed-in rocker studs. In the "far-out" performance category are connecting rod and piston kits used on the high-performance engines. The connecting rod is heavier and has a larger diameter wrist pin. Pistons are eyebrowed for added relief from lift of the high performance cam shaft. This notching is necessary to allow space during the valve overlap period so pistons won't tag valves when at top dead center.

Until early 1964 all Shelby American racing cars used a standard Ford high performance cam. Ford designed it on a computer and it worked out extremely well. This, the exact cam used in production versions of the 289-cubic-inch V-8, is so good that Shelby's racing Cobras were able to use it. By modifying cylinder heads and revising carburetion, engine tuners at Shelby American increased horsepower and torque of the engine to undreamed of heights. Eventually it was decided to sacrifice some low-end power in favor of a modified camshaft moving the horsepower and torque curve higher into the RPM range. New racing Cobras have sacrificed 15 to 20 horsepower in the lower RPM ranges and added it at the top end. This was done in the early Cooper-Cobra and the Daytona Cobra to improve high speed performance and put horsepower and torque peaks at the higher speeds where they are being used to a better advantage.

Early in 1964 Shelby American announced a series of changes to their Cobra after nearly 21 months of production. Only visible sign of change was a set of air vents just back of the front wheels to purge the engine compartment of excess heat and assist both engine cooling and comfort for driver and passenger. The 1964 Cobra also boasted other cooling devices. They were aluminum air shrouds protecting the passenger foot box and the battery. The shrouds added to the air vents—located just back of the front wheels—solved overheat problems of earlier models. The shroud between the battery and exhaust headers increases life of the high capacity, premium grade battery that is standard equipment in the street Cobra.

In the 1964 Cobra an alternator has replaced the generator. This is the most significant change in the all-new electrical system. The alternator is preferred because it allows battery charge during normal idle and is a more efficient, complete

Americanization of the electrical system. Wiring looms are now supplied by Ford. Heavy duty Stewart-Warner instruments are in the cockpit. Autolite supplies batteries and spark plugs.

A new tire was developed for the production car driver. High horsepower-to-weight ratio of the powerful sports car created a tire problem that was solved by introduction of the G-8 Goodyear. Features of the new tire are its excellent wet weather properties and resistance to "roll over" on the edges during cornering. Improved braking systems included a new automatically adjusting emergency brake. The Girling disc brakes have been improved, and pads with greater surface contact and pressure have been installed. Dual master cylinders are now a part of the front and rear brake systems to provide independent operation. Technically, Girling front calipers have been changed over from Type 16-P to the improved 16-3, and rear calipers remain 12-3 HPs, but with addition of the self-adjusting emergency brake pad and mechanism. Front disc thickness has been increased from $\frac{1}{2}$ inch to $\frac{5}{8}$ inch, and rear disc thickness from $\frac{3}{8}$ inch to $\frac{1}{2}$ inch.

Sway bar brackets have been added to A arm and frame members in the suspension. This improvement allows "do-it-yourself" Cobra owners to install sway bars without having to ship their cars back to the factory. Foot pedals are easier to reach because they have been moved farther from the transmission tunnel and farther apart from each other. Hood latches have been improved. Fastenings are now secured better to prevent hood buffeting at high speeds. An improved transmission, dubbed the "Sebring transmission," is now available with a closer ratio between third and fourth gears.

The relationship between the Shelby American people and their co-production workers of A.C. Cars Ltd., of England, has been extremely satisfactory. Nevertheless, problems have arisen and been successfully compromised. One of the more unusual was that of identifying the car. As originally conceived and built, it was the Shelby-A.C.-Ford-Cobra, rather a long tongue-twisting name. A.C. felt logically that the body and chassis was an A.C., and Shelby American people believed that the car was a Shelby Cobra. Ford felt they ought to have their name on the car. For practicability something finally had to give. People just couldn't say this name. Were a dealer to advertise the car on the radio, it would take half an hour merely to identify it. Finally, among Shelby American people, it was cut down to the point of being called the Ford Cobra.

Still, A.C. felt that this car was an A.C., and they put their A.C. emblem on the trunk and hood. The A.C. emblem was rather large and had to be attached with prongs through sheet metal. When cars arrived in Venice, one of the first things Shelby American mechanics did was take the A.C. emblem off and apply the Cobra tag made up by Shelby American. It didn't even have a snake on it—just "Shelby Cobra" in the middle of which was a small A.C. emblem. Metal finishers would install pop rivets in the holes left from the English tag, grind them down and repaint before putting the Cobra emblem on the panel. After a month or two the paint would shrink and harden and the pop rivet would begin to show.

Obviously Shelby American needed a new emblem. The artist, overwhelmed by the word Cobra, created a snake emblem of such size and design as to be something less than pleasing to the beholder. The lettering was a style long out of fashion and was off center.

It was decided to completely redesign the emblem. Fortunately, by then A.C. agreed to eliminate attachment of their emblems on the panels. Rivet holes thus no longer were a problem, and it was possible to create a neat emblem fitting panels in the proper position. Ford Motor Company's identification requirements were satisfied by attaching a small "Ford Powered" emblem on the right and left cowl panels just behind the front wheels.

Shel's "Dream Come True"

I really don't care about selling the Cobra to just anyone. What I'm trying to build is a sports car for the true sport car enthusiast. I couldn't care less about selling cars to someone that needs a car with power windows and wants to look like a sport.

I am interested in selling cars to people who really and truly are connoisseurs of sports cars. That's the main reason I hold production down. I'm really trying not to build more than I can sell. I always want to have a demand for many more cars than I can build. Right now I have that.

I originally built the Cobra with the Ford engine and transmission because I believe it's silly to have a car sitting in the garage waiting for a little 15-cent part to be flown in from Italy. I think you should be able to go to your automobile dealer in this country and pick up any parts you need. That was my basic reason for the American engine. I don't think I need to give a Cobra owner any advice other than what's in the service manual. We don't have a car that's temperamental. Our drive train is strong enough and you'll never have any problems with the engine.

Strangely enough, if we do have a customer problem, it's with people over-revving the engines. Father buys a Cobra and lets sonny take it out. We tell them that 7,000 rpm is the limit. When you go past that you're going to drop a valve. The springs just won't take it. Invariably that's what happens. The boy will shuck an engine and swear that he never got near the 7,000 mark. So far we've never lost any engines except for this thing.

There is no need to be too respectful of this car. Cobra owners know they've got the fastest accelerating sports car and consequently most of them drive it the same way. There's not anything to tell anyone except to have fun with it. The only limitation I like to make about a Cobra is "Drive as rough and ready as you want to but don't over-rev the engine." I'm not afraid of anything else.

Because I've never intended to build more than say 500 cars a year, I don't have any plans for changing the Cobra for a couple of years. Pretty soon, I'll have a racing team of Cobras and may develop a working company. Now we've

During 1963, Shelby American driver Dave McDonald (center) was presented with the "Helm's Sportsman of the Year" award.

developed a Cobra Kit which is hop-up and speed equipment for all lines of Ford passenger cars. It can be used in road racing, on a drag strip, or just for fun driving on the street.

I have my driving school which I intend to expand and hope to have a race track under construction in 1964. I have a lot of plans. I want to get myself in a position where I build a car with my heart rather than trying to build it for profit. I want to build what I think is the best sports car in the world, that sells at a decent price, and will out-perform any other car for the money involved.

2. A. C. Cars, the Specialist Builders

A.C. Cars Ltd., at Thames Ditton near Kingston-upon-Thames in Surrey, about 12 miles from London, is typical of many specialist car works that abounded in England before and after World War II. Now they are disappearing under impact of market flooding by the Big Five: the British Motor Corporation, Vauxhall, Ford, Triumph and the Rootes Group.

A.C. has gone through many phases, its present role being that of builder of a "hand made" sports type car. An association which commenced in 1900 between John Portwine and John Weller is responsible for the A.C. They joined hands to produce a rather unconventional vehicle known as the Weller car. Mr. Weller in his early twenties designed the unusual automobile in which the 20-horsepower engine, gear box, radiator and muffler were assembled on an underframe. This was suspended to three points on the main chassis, which prevented torsional strain and shifting of the chassis frame from being transmitted to the power and drive units. The completed car was exhibited in the 1903 Motor Show at Crystal Palace in London.

Business management of A.C. was in the hands of Portwine, by trade a butcher owning a chain of shops in South London. It was Portwine who realized that production difficulties in building the Weller car, and mounting costs, might make it more desirable to do something for the commercial market. His idea of building commercial vehicles was responsible for the title Autocarrier coming into existence when the firm was known as Auto, Car and Accessories Limited. Their first vehicle was a tricycle affair with two wheels in front and a single wheel in back. The rear wheel was driven by a 5.6

horsepower single-cylinder aircooled engine. Steering was by a tiller on which was mounted brake and throttle. These units were highly successful. In London, Autocarriers were replacing horsedrawn delivery vans as rapidly as they could be purchased. As the history of A.C. company says, "The vehicles being robust and simple to control were able to stand up to the severe conditions imposed by London traffic which was thick and heavy even in those days. They were mostly handled by youths of 17 years. In that age the spirit of adventure thrived on the roads and as traffic bluebottles were less in evidence than they are today the boys were inclined to race every other Autocarrier they met. The fact that the vehicles stood up to this kind of treatment speaks volumes."

By 1907 passenger cars entered the field and a new company, called Autocarriers Limited, was formed. This firm absorbed the entire Autocarrier interest of Auto, Car and Accessories Limited with Portwine and Weller remaining as directors of the new company. Three passenger car models were eventually produced, one for a driver behind the passenger, another for a driver and two passengers, and a third with the driver and passenger side by side in the front seat. The price of the new car at that time was £90 or approximately $400.00. Instruction books issued with these early passenger cars were extremely explicit. Owners were advised, "If you should have any difficulties just at first, don't blame the machine. Remember it has passed very severe tests at the hands of experts before it was delivered. Quietly read through these hints to find out where your trouble lies."

During the World War I a number of these three-wheeled tricycle affairs were used by the British Army to transport troops and machine guns. Following conclusion of the war the factory began producing a four wheeled car of Weller design. Though it is not known if Weller was the inventor, one of the first single plate clutches fitted to a British car was on the early A.C. sports roadster. Another unique feature was that the transmission, differential and rear wheel brake were all mounted as a single unit. In effect the rear brake stopped

During World War I the British Army experimented with "Cyclist" troops mounted on three-wheeled vehicles mad by Autocarriers, Ltd. This parent company, of A.C. Cars, Ltd., built these vehicles for machine gun and light cannon mounting. (Chapter Two, Pg. 5)

the drive shaft from turning which effectively controlled activity at rear wheels.

The first of the A.C. four-wheeled cars were delivered in 1919 with a four-cylinder French engine. Later, a British Four was used. Finally, in 1919, A.C. Cars began to produce the first light six. This optional power unit weighed less than 350 pounds, notwithstanding use of a cast iron cylinder head and steel flywheel. This weight included both the starter and the generator. Much of the engine block and crankcase were cast of aluminum.

Early A.C. cars, with their six-cylinder engine, were extremely reliable and active in record breaking. By the end of 1921, A.C. held over one hundred records at Brooklands race track; four times more than any other car which com-

31

peted in its class. On April 7, 1922, an A. C. broke the 6 to 12 hours record at speed of 68.52 miles per hour and established records for 400 to 800 miles at 69.18 miles per hour, all from a standing start. These records were achieved with a special A.C. four-cylinder overhead-valve engine which had four valves per cylinder.

On November 24 at Brooklands, in 1922, a single seater A.C. broke a number of existing light car records and gained all 1500cc records with the exception of 50 miles and 50 kilometers which it held. The little car was timed over the flying half mile at 108.4 miles an hour and ran ten miles at 103.79 miles an hour—this in 1922 from a 1500cc engine. By 1923 the six-cylinder cars were outdistancing the four under the direction of Mr. S. F. Edge who joined the company in February of '21. The founders of A.C., Portwine and Weller, had resigned from the company in 1922, following disagreements with Edge over company policy matters.

The company was re-registered in 1927 as A.C. (Acedes) Cars Limited, with S. F. Edge in control. Typical English limited-production cars were built including open roadsters, coupes, long wheel base coupes, touring cars, a sedan with fabric body, a sedan with a coach-built body and a Victoria-type coupe on a short chassis. In 1929 financial difficulties beset the company and production shut down. Only the service department remained open to care for cars still running on the road.

Late in 1929 the company was brought to the attention of the Hurlock brothers. W. E. F. Hurlock took over as managing director for the corporation and his brother, Charles, became general manager. They had purchased all the assets of A.C., along with equipment and spare parts. When they first contemplated purchase of the bankrupt business, late in '29, their idea was to use the premises to dispose of vast amounts of war surplus (World War I) still on the market.

In surveying the premises they were surprised to find a large number of chassis frames, engines and other parts in the warehouse—"for free" as it were. They decided, after purchasing A.C. Cars, to assemble what there was and give the motor manufacturing business a "go." Fortunately it worked out well and the A.C. car remained in production. At this time the company had three plants. One, which is in use today, is the Taggs Island premises. A second was the Ferry Works on the side of the River Thames next door to the ancient Swan Hostelry. The latter premises had been used for balloon storage during World War I.

The Taggs Island plant is just what the name suggests— an island in the middle of the River Thames. By air, it is only about a half a mile from the main A.C. Thames Ditton Works; but as access has to be gained by a bridge from the main Hampton Kings Road, a drive of about three miles is necessary. Total area of the plants is 130,000 square feet. It is a most unusual factory site. On the same island is a large hotel, restaurant, the Casino, a well known spot near London for drinking and dancing. During the last war (World War II), the Hurlock brothers had to buy the Casino to retain possession of their factory. It stayed in their hands until about two years ago when the hotel was sold to an outside enterprise.

The Taggs Island factory was responsible for a series of electric railway cars built for the Southend Corporation and a group of Leyland diesel-engined single-carriage rail cars manufactured for the British Railways. The rail cars were designed for use where curved radius was not too abrupt. The chassis used four wheels with no bogies. Since the rail cars would not be subjected to pushing about in marshaling yards, the A.C. company designed them so that the finished cars were 600 pounds lighter than specifications. As a result they had performance in excess of expectations.

The first post-war A.C. car left the factory in October of 1947. This was a two-door sedan of extremely modern appearance, full-flared fenders sweeping low over the front with running boards more a decorative feature than a useful device. This A.C. was powered by a three-carburetor, overhead-cam, in-line six-cylinder engine which had long been a feature of all A.C. cars. The car had semi-elliptic leaf springs and solid axles both front and rear. It was equipped with hydraulic brakes in front and mechanical rears to provide necessary braking for increased speed of the vehicle. It went out of production in 1954.

One of the senior executives of A.C. Cars Limited, sales manager R. G. "Jock" Henderson, joined the company in 1927. He came down from Scotland and started with A.C. working with machinery. Before long he was test driving and in a number of years was made sales manager. Before and after World War II he drove A.C. cars at rallies and was responsible for publicity and advertising. Recently he wrote "The History of A.C. Cars Limited." Currently he doesn't have anything to "sell," for the entire A.C. output is Cobras which have been sold to Carroll Shelby. The show room, in which his office is situated, is now the delivery bay. Here new Cobras await Customs inspection and pickup by four-car transporters. From the A.C. factory they are trucked to London's Victoria docks where they are shipped off to Shelby American in the United States. As shipped, the Cobras weigh only 1,400 pounds and lack an engine or gear box, which serves to demonstrate A.C.'s light weight yet massive construction. Loading is done with the aid of forklift trucks.

Until just a few years ago, A.C. Cars was one of very few small British specialist car manufacturers to completely make their own engine. Since 1919, Weller's "Light Six" had been capable of improvement to keep it in line and ahead of power plants of other concerns. Weller, a man of great designing skill, was a forward thinker of a high order. Though he conceived the Light Six shortly after World War I, its specifications are still regarded as up-to-date. In fact, English designers consider it ahead of many current six-cylinder engines. It had an aluminum alloy block, wet cylinder liners and a single overhead cam shaft. Pictures of this light-six engine show it to be highly similar to the die cast aluminum overhead-valve six used by Rambler in 1961, and 1962. The 120-cubic-inch A.C. engine weighed about 350 pounds in spite of using a cast-iron cylinder head. In 1961 the same basic engine was still an available power plant unit for the Ace, the open two-seater Tojeiro-based car from which the Cobra evolved. It was producing 103 horsepower at 4,500 rpm. But need for higher and higher performance had made the A.C. company look elsewhere for an optional power unit long before this.

After World War II, during England's austerity period, great numbers of the A.C. Petite were sold. It was a development of an "invalid carriage" made by A.C. for the War Ministry. The Petite, with two wheels in back, one in front, is a two passenger vehicle powered by a rear-mounted single-cylinder two-stroke engine of 346 c.c.

The beginning of the Cobra was around 1950. Sedans, touring cars, invalid carriages, electric trains and other products of the A.C. factory kept both plants busy. But the Hurlock brothers and their management people were keenly aware of the great awakening of motoring as a sport in Europe and America. They were highly concerned about producing a really fast sports car to bear the name A.C. Their "evergreen" Light Six was still capable of producing more power and its light weight made it very desirable for good handling and high performance characteristics of a sports car.

It was increasingly obvious that the A.C. channel type chassis frame was becoming outmoded in sports car design. Use of solid axles was also a thing of the past in high quality, high performance categories; although Ferrari, Alfa Romeo and a few others hung on to non-independent rear ends for a long time.

This is the Tojeiro prototype, powered with a Bristol six. Cliff Davis is driving, in this picture taken in 1952, one year before the A.C. Ace was announced.

At Gatewood, Cliff Davis, in the Tojeiro-Bristol, is chased by a Le Mans replica Frazer-Nash. Both cars had the same engine (1952) but the Tojeiro-Bristol was the first of the new school of sports car design.

During this period a Bristol-engined six-cylinder sports car called a Tojeiro was enjoying immense success in national and international races. It was driven by a London automobile dealer "Cliff" Davis. The car had been designed by John Tojeiro, a young Englishman of Portuguese descent. He had used simple but established principles to build an outstandingly good, fast and sturdy vehicle. The frame principle was similar to the pre-war Mercedes-Benz Grand Prix cars. The chassis structure in the main consisted of two steel tubes of large diameter. These longerons were joined by welded tubular cross members. Further stiffness was built into the frame by welding a tubular hoop in the cowl area. All four wheels of the Tojeiro car were independently sprung by transverse leaf springs and wishbones. As race meets showed, braking and handling were remarkably good for such a simple layout.

When the A.C. Ace was introduced, in 1953, the chromed and painted chassis was displayed. In 1953, the Ace was one of two British cars with independent rear suspension. The other, Lagonda's 2.6, is no longer in production.

English motoring journalists were quick to point out that it did not need much of an engineering analysis to deduce that the Tojeiro suspension system was more or less a carbon copy of the arrangement used on the Cooper 500cc racing car. This Cooper design later grew into the Formula 2 and later Formula 1 machines. However, as Cooper had borrowed the scheme from pre-and post-war Fiat 500s, one can hardly direct any sort of criticism at Tojeiro. What happened was, that Coopers, when building their first 500cc racing car, had looked around for an easy-to-adapt, all-independent-suspension system for their ultra-lightweight single-cylinder baby. They hit on the brilliant idea of taking two Fiat front suspensions and using them fore and aft of a strengthened Fiat 500 chassis frame. The resultant Cooper was a sensation and ultimately led to the configuration of modern rear engine Grand Prix cars.

Both cars have the same basic engine, the "Light Six" designed by A.C. The older car is a 1927-29 model A.C., the roadster is an early Ace, also powered by the "Light Six" though of some 500 c.c. larger displacement than the engine in the 1927-29 model.

A.C. realized that the Tojeiro-Bristol, an excellent race proved design, could be a good new sports car bearing their name. John Tojeiro sold A.C. the manufacturing rights of that type, and in 1953 the beautiful A.C. Ace began to gain a following among sporting motorists. It was a highly successful car in British club racing—being the type of fast, tough car that a private owner could race and rally, then use it for his ordinary everyday motoring. This was the type of owner that A.C. tried to accommodate for many years. And this was the basis for Carroll Shelby's Cobra.

Many famous English drivers, such as Ken Rudd, John Dalton and others, were driving Aces in competition. It soon became obvious that a more powerful model would be desirable for those who wanted maximum performance for road work, racing, or both. At that time (1956) the car division of the Bristol Aeroplane Company was still manufacturing a 2-liter six cylinder engine for its range of high performance sedans.

In 1956, A.C. contacted Bristol and expressed interest in buying the famed Bristol Six for use in A.C.'s line of coupes and roadsters. The story behind Bristol's series of 2-liter engines is unique, as it involves both Germany and England and more than one car maker. Before World War II there was an extremely fast and highly successful German sports car made by the Bavarian firm of BMW (Bayerische Motoren Werken) designated as Type 328. This car had a profound influence on subsequent sports car design, as it demonstrated the desirability of an efficient aero-dynamic shape to extract 100 miles an hour performance with relatively low power output. It also showed the necessity of independent front suspension to gain necessary handling and road holding.

The BMW 2-Liter six cylinder sports car notched up a tremendous string of successes in racing trials and rallies in the 30's. It was an extremely clever design propelled by an 85 horsepower engine which had been evolved from an ordinary push rod overhead valve production power plant. The basic engine had been in production since 1932 when BMW's chief designer, a Dr. Fiedler, was requested to develop a sports car engine from production components. He did not follow the typical route of raising compression ratio, fitting larger valves, special cam shafts and multiple carburetors. Instead, he designed a completely new cylinder head which transformed the original engine. His was a cylinder head of great ingenuity.

Dr. Fiedler's new cylinder head was designed to provide nearly all advantages of twin overhead camshafts and hemispherical combustion chambers without expense and high production cost usually found for such a power unit. Overhead valves were set at an angle of 80 degrees in the hemispherical combustion chamber. They were actuated by rockers which were in turn levered by crossover push rods and rockers from a single crankcase located camshaft. Thus with the single camshaft of the touring engine and ingenious system of push rods, rockers and secondary rockers, the production based engine was transformed into a potent sports unit. Due to the valve system, a most efficient form of down draft carburetor inlets was incorporated in the head. Three downdraft carburetors could be advantageously used.

In England, H. J. Aldington of Frazer-Nash Cars Limited

had been building a chain-driven sports car for more than ten years. He was aware of the incredible performance and competition reliability of the BMW power plant. Though he kept his chain driven cars in production until 1938, from '34 he took on distributorship of BMW cars in England. All imported touring and sports models of the BMW were fitted with a right hand drive at Aldington's works near London. They were marketed in England under the name of Frazer-Nash-BMW. The Frazer-Nash people also did much to further develop reliability of the German cars. Aldington, besides many other great drivers, made the 328's nearly invincible in the 2-Liter class in racing, rallies, hill climbs, and so forth. By 1939 some of his competition models were producing well over a 110 brake horsepower.

After World War II, Aldington was quick to realize that BMW would take some time to get on their commercial feet, and when that happened they would probably require a completely different sort of power plant. He went to Germany and approached BMW for rights to manufacture their engine. As he had been a good friend of the BMW people in pre-war days, they readily agreed. Aldington needed a post-war engine for his Frazer-Nash sports car which by then had become a potent 120 mile an hour machine with normal shaft drive to the rear axle. He knew he couldn't afford to manufacture the the BMW engine himself, so Aldington convinced the Bristol Aeroplane Company that they should get into car building. He would get the design and production know how for the 328 engine and Bristol would build it for him and for themselves.

The resulting cooperative venture worked well. Not only did Bristol have an engine of outstanding merit and performance but Frazer-Nash got an engine for their sports car that exceeded expectations. The Bristol engine not only powered their own range of expensive cars but was found under the hoods of Frazer-Nash, Cooper, Tojeiro, ERA, Lister, Kieft in both sports and racing categories. Frazer-Nash achieved a fantastic run of international successes with a win in the Sebring 12 hours, a Third at LeMans, two Thirds in the Tourist Trophy, Third in the Prix d' Monte Carlo and a win in the grueling Targa Florio, the only British car to win this Siciliian classic.

By the time A.C. came to an arrangement with Bristol Aeroplane Company, about use of the engine in the Ace, it was possible to have 140 brake horsepower output. As sold in the production model, the power plant was 128 horsepower at 5,500 rpm. The Ace "Light Six" engine remained in production and was made an option in the Ace at less cost. The first Ace Bristol was completed in March, 1956, by which time the charming Aceca coupe was in production (since 1955) with an option of either engine.

The A.C. Aceca coupe, introduced with the Ace roadster in 1953. Front sheet metal, chassis and power plant are identical to the roadster. Only rear deck and top differ. Early coupe models were noted for water leaks, a problem soon solved by A.C. engineers.

In November of 1958, the AUTOCAR, a well regarded British Motoring Journal, tested the A.C. Ace Bristol. Here's what they had to say about it. "Fast without temperament, light without fragility, modern without extremism, the A.C. Ace is a traditional British sports car brought up to date. For those to whom really rapid motoring is a recreation, the A.C. Ace

Bristol offers a most rewarding combination of sheer speed and acceleration with very safe handling, superb brakes and first class steering."

Even at the time, the Ace Bristol was a hot car. Standard acceleration times were 0 to 60 in 7.4 seconds. This with a six cylinder engine rated at 125 horsepower. Total weight of the car was 1,845 pounds. Maximum speed was 117 miles an hour. Certainly no little indication of the reason Carroll Shelby chose this vehicle as the bed in which to mate the powerful Ford Fairlane V-8.

According to Jock Henderson of the Thames Ditton factory, the first letter from Carroll Shelby outlining his proposal, was received September 8, 1961. Carroll liked the robust look of the tubular chassis coupled with the traditional high finish and hand-made reputation of the A.C. cars. These he thought, were the basis of the type of sports car discerning Americans would like to buy—particularly since an American engine, gear box and instrumentation would solve the problems of servicing and spare parts.

A.C. management realized the wisdom of the proposal and two Ford V8 engines were shipped from the U.S. in October, 1961. A. C. soon proved that one of the highly pleasing design points of the Ace was a massive underhood space. It was found that the engine would drop in with room to spare for efficient exhaust manifolding. There were few installation problems. The Ford engine and Borg-Warner gear box were mated with the British-made Salisbury rear end—a well known differential unit. When set up for the Ace, it was mounted solidly to the rear of the chassis from where it drove rear wheels through universally jointed stub shafts.

The prototype A.C.-Cobra was put together during the winter of 1961-62. It was considered an "assembly exercise" by A.C. "We did drive the thing up the road," says Jock Henderson, "to see that everything worked, but time was short." Engine and gear box were removed and the prototype chassis flown to the U.S. It left Thames Ditton on February 16, 1962, three months after work began.

Development was then carried on by Shelby, who had Ford of Dearborn working with him. Considering that the chassis was handling nearly 100 more hp than it ever had before, snags proved few and far between. It was found that carriers for the final drive were breaking under the enormous V8 torque. This was traced to the fact that rear stub shaft splines were locking when power was being put to rear wheels. Contributing to this was a degree of chassis flexing which was soon put to right. Gauge of chassis tubing wall was increased and the final drive casting was mounted with rubber bushings. After more than 40 years of relatively small capacity engines, A.C. test drivers had been amazed by the torque of a 289 V8 engine. Jock Henderson says, "There's torque everywhere. It will run up to about 7000 rpm, yet at slow speeds and in high gear it will dart away at the touch of the throttle."

In 1963 two A.C. Cobras were entered at Le Mans. One belonged to the Hugus-Shelby alliance and was a product of the Shelby American group. The second was entered by A.C. Cars Ltd. Both groups were responsible for their own race preparation. In this instance, A.C. built up their car complete for the 24-hour classic. The British-entered car was sponsored by a London newspaper and the drivers were Peter Bolton and Ninian Sanderson, the latter a Scotsman who had won the race in 1956, in a Jaguar. Both entries were team managed by Stirling Moss, and A.C. speaks most highly of his pit management. The factory car was prepared at Thames Ditton, with all pre-race high speed running and testing carried on at MIRA, the British motor industry's research and test ground at Nuneaton, England.

A.C. factory people say that the engine they were supplied with from Dearborn was very much a "cooking" (ordinary) model of standard specification and tune. In spite of its moderate power output, their car was extremely fast. The works did all its testing, planning and gearing to suit 6.50" section rear tires. These, they understood, would be supplied for the race. When the A.C. factory team arrived at Le Mans they were informed by the tire manufacturers that 7-inch rear tires would be used which of course abused the rear axle ratio. This, plus the fact that the British car's engine was considered relatively a non-eager-beaver, made A.C.'s entry slower than planned.

In retrospect, A.C. people agree that the "cooking engine" and overloading of the tires may have reduced the car's potential only slightly. However, it easily played an important part in conserving the car's stamina. It ran seventh and was the first car home after the winning Ferraris. In so doing, the Bolton-Sanderson Cobra averaged 108 miles per hour and covered 2592 miles.

When A.C. dismantled the engine after the race, they found it like new inside. All they did, before reassembling the Ford Fairlane V8, was to touch up valve faces. According to A.C. mechanics, they did this not from necessity but because it seemed a pity to dismantle the engine and not do something to it. The car entered by Shelby retired after running slightly more than 9-$\frac{1}{2}$ hours. Three different stories claim to account for the retirement. One blames a burnt piston, the second a broken piston and the third tells of a broken connecting rod.

As to performance, the Bolton-Sanderson car was timed at 161 miles an hour on the straightaway, and the Hugus-Jopp at 160. One of the surprising facts which came to light during Le Mans practice was the tendency for a rear window to be sucked out of the hardtop used on the Cobras. This was cured by securing windows with screws, but it brings into sharp focus the fact that aerodynamics of the Cobra body were not as good as they might be.

A.C. Cars Ltd. production today is concentrated on the Cobra. The A.C. machine shop produces steering shafts, suspension parts and the entire center-lock hubs for the wire wheels; including costly splining of the hubs. Even the radiator grille is hand-made. After it is riveted together, by an A.C. craftsman, it is sent to a sub-contractor for anodizing.

Main chassis tubes and cross-members are arc-welded into a solid assembly in the main assembly room of the Thames Ditton factory. Nearby the body framing and support brackets

Chassis frames, of welded construction using both square and round tubing, are mounted on dollys for easy handling in the A.C. shop.

Chassis assembly line has frames, in distance, "dressed" with brakes, springs and other fittings for the Cobra.

45

Once off the chassis assembly line, partially completed Cobras are stored in the Service Shop of A.C. Cars Ltd. Four Cobras awaiting installation of the aluminum body shell.

Each car is hand-sanded before the first coat of primer. Hand-sanding follows each application of paint until the final coat of coach quality color is applied.

Two at a time, on flat-bed trailers, engineless Cobras begin their journey to the U. S.

are added to the chassis tubes by gas welding. The chassis and framing are built of mild steel, in a mixed framework of round and square tubing which contributes to stiffness of the structure. Though such a simple "two tube" structure is often accused of being out of date, automotive engineers have much good to say about the Cobra chassis. It is simple to build, resists corrosion well and allows fitting of doors without weakening the frame. For small production runs, such as the Cobra, this type of structure is more economical than space-frames or monocoque construction.

All body-panel work is done outside the Thames-Ditton works. Two sub-contractors work aluminum sheet into formed body panels which are assembled at Thames Ditton and the body completed for installation over the chassis tube frame. Production increases were, in the beginning, almost more than A.C. could handle but as of January 1964, a handmade, engine-less, gearbox-less car is built at the rate of 15 a week for Shelby American.

3. Production—A Climb for Quality

A rather unfortunate accident, in the last race in which Shelby's Cobra used a 260 V-8, took place at Daytona, Florida, in February, 1963. Shelby's mechanics and drivers had planned an all-out effort on the high-speed Daytona track with four of the finest cars Shelby could build. Two new chassis had the latest rack and pinion steering and two were running the older worm and sector system. Unfortunately they were dogged with a strange series of accidents which threw two cars out of the race and left Dave McDonald to finish fourth.

Skip Hudson was running well ahead of less efficient competition when he coasted into the pit with his fuel line broken. Mechanics quickly replaced the broken tubing and sent him back out again. The engine was running perfectly but no one had noticed that the V-8's harmonic balancer, attached to the front of the crankshaft, had come apart. A small portion of it had ruptured the fuel line. After a few laps at 140 to 150 miles an hour Hudson found himself in trouble. At this speed vibration frequencies of the Fairlane V-8 were no longer damped out by the broken harmonic balancer. All of a sudden harmonics built up to engine destroying pitch and the clutch exploded. One section tore up through the clutch housing, broke Hudson's right foot on the accelerator, continued through the foot box in the passenger compartment, hit the steering column and bent it three inches out of line.

The steering locked and Skip could do nothing with the bent column. Though he got the car slowed, it slammed against the guard rail going over 50 miles an hour. Riding down the guard rail in a burst of dust and noisy fury, Hudson left the race (and racing) for the season.

The original vibration damper on the front of the 260 V-8 crankshaft was made with a malleable cast-iron pulley ring. It was attached to the bonded rubber disc of the crankshaft damper. This cast iron ring broke and harmonic vibrations in the engine caused the clutch to fail. Unknown to Shelby mechanics, Ford engineers had already been working on a change for this critical part. They had developed a different type of front pulley and damper for their production cars. When production of the 289-cubic-inch Ford V-8 began, for the '63-½ vehicles, the pulley was almost twice the width of the original unit on the 260. Instead of being a casting, it is made of stamped steel. Not a true damper, the steel stamping is a far more satisfactory part which has never caused any problem during the most severe competition a Cobra engine has been subjected to. By then the 289 V-8 had been announced in two versions. One was the standard 289 for production cars. The other was a special high performance powerplant, the first of which were available in Shelby's Cobra. Many things learned from Carroll Shelby's experimentation with the 260 V-8 were carried into the 289. In addition to the steel harmonic balancer the clutch was changed, rod and connecting bearings were of new material, and cylinder heads had been modified. Valve design was changed and instead of a valve train with hydraulic lifters, the 289 high-performance version was equipped with solid lifters which allowed higher rpms and higher maximum output. Rocker studs were screwed into the heads instead of being pressed in. There was better bearing material and better balance on the front counterweight. This more powerful, sporting engine could be installed in Cobras without change at the Cobra factory.

Big improvements were more than simply bore and stroke because the 289 design was basically the same as the 260. Instead, the 260 had been refined and brought up to a peak of perfection which was shortly to make the 289 V-8 felt in competition throughout the world.

The severe heating problem that early Cobras were plagued with had been solved in a series of unique moves. The first cars to come through from England were equipped with an English Ford Zephyr radiator. It was completely inadequate. About the time Shelby began installing Ford's 289 V-8, efforts to find a new radiator had become successful. McCord Radiator Co., a prime vendor for the Ford Division, agreed to make a radiator to Carroll Shelby's specifications. They also produced header tanks which eliminated all cooling system fabrication work previously necessary in the production of Carroll Shelby's Cobra.

Another change proved desirable by Daytona racing experience was modification to production steering systems. All early Cobras were equipped with a worm and sector steering which had a lengthy idler arm and two track rods to each steering arm. This system was, by racing car standards, quite complicated. Shelby mechanics were sure their car would handle better if the steering were revised. They had found that toe-in changed during wheel travel. This put such a severe load on the idler arm's ball joints that the idler arm bracket failed during competition due to the relative inefficiency of the worm and sector system. Now, as a result of racing experience, all current Cobras are produced with rack and pinion steering which has reduced the number of parts and eliminated failures during competition.

It's worth noting that in this improvement, A.C. Cars realized the shortcomings of their own front end. The revised rack and pinion steering was developed by them, as a production standard, for fitting to Carroll Shelby's Cobra.

One other change to production cars accruing from race development, was in the starter mechanism of the 289 V-8. A small aluminum box in the starter contained an assembly of retainers, washers and collars which held field segments of the starter. Under rough and continuous running of competition, the field segments were rattling themselves to pieces. During a pit stop, a Cobra driver could find he had no starter and was out of the race. Shelby mechanics took it upon themselves to remedy the situation and came up with what they thought was a fairly good "fix." In consultation with Ford engineers, the Shelby American modification to the starter was eventually approved for all Ford production engines.

A.C. Cars Ltd. has benefited from Shelby's race research too. In the first race the Cobra entered, when it was leading at Riverside, California, in October of 1962, a failure in the left rear axle hub put it out of the race. Within a few days Shelby chief engineer, Phil Remington, developed a forging to replace the standard AC axle hub. The highly stressed part was modified with new radii in some critical areas plus an increase in tensile strength of the material. This solved breakage problems and the part has subsequently been made a standard by AC.

Another early problem encountered in racing Cobras was the differential mounting brackets. Originally malleable iron castings, three or four of them failed during early Cobra racing efforts. To get out of the woods, Shelby American mechanics made new differential brackets out of 4130 steel tubing and plate stock, arc welded together and normalized to eliminate internal stresses of fabrication. Since then AC has created a forging of extreme durability for the brackets.

Though the head gasket of a stock 289 Ford V-8 was quite satisfactory for normal use, racing speeds and constant heat soon melted off the crimped steel edge. Once that burned away, extreme pressures of competition driving caused the gasket to blow. Ford engineers came up with a shim steel gasket similar to that used on the Ford high-performance 427-cubic-inch V-8. This gasket uses no asbestos at all. It relies on stamped sections, and accuracy of construction for its sealing. Ken Miles started one racing season on an engine equipped with the new shim steel gasket and drove it over 7,000 racing miles with the gaskets holding firm—proof, more than anything else, that racing and competition do much to improve the quality of production engines.

Cobras 1 to 70 were equipped with a Lucas (English) electrical system. Though completely satisfactory for most use, it would fail to keep the battery charged during long periods of traffic driving. More than one Cobra owner found himself without a battery to start his car because the Lucas generator did not charge sufficiently at idle. Cars 71 to 200 were equipped with a Ford generator of higher capacity. After car 200 the electrical system of all Cobras was completely Ford with an alternator, reducing drag on the engine and providing maximum battery charge at idle.

Early customers complained that cockpits of their cars became so hot in summertime that it was a question of baking feet or driving at excessive speeds in order to provide circulation of air. It wasn't long before AC cars of England was installing ducting from the front of the car directly into the cockpit to cool it during hot days. Oringinal windshields were not too well secured to the body and early Cobras treated their owners to quite a bit of shake and rattle in the cowl area. Cobra production engineer Leonard Parsons developed a gusset which could be fitted up underneath the cowl to provide a more secure windshield mounting and additional bolts were added on each side.

Comparison of Shelby's prototype (left) with 1964 production Cobra on right shows how trunk lid was shortened to stiffen body section behind rear bumper.

It's obvious from a comparison of early- and late-model Cobras that there has been a change in the deck lid opening. The section of body paneling below the deck lid opening has been increased in depth to provide additional rigidity for the rear deck. Though the deck lid is slightly smaller than before, it is of no consequence—there is plenty of room for loading or removal of luggage and spare tire. In early cars the gas tank was below the spare tire, in effect a portion of the trunk floor. Shelby American chief engineer Phil Remington had the tank moved to a vertical position over the rear axle, behind the driver. The spare tire now sits in a tire well, made of fiberglass, in the area where the gas tank was before. A cover over it provides a smooth floor for luggage. From Remington's point of view, and that of competition drivers, the gas tank over the rear axle is a much more suitable mounting. As the tank empties, there is less effect on handling of the car than when weight changes take place at the extreme rear.

1964 Cobra trunk area shows central gas tank filler, and tank mounted over the rear axle, behind the passenger compartment. Section of A.C. tube frame at left side of trunk.

Other modifications made by A.C. in England, and now appearing on production cars, include a unique hood latch with finger-type wing nuts. This allows the car owner to open the hood without use of the "T" handle key that was needed for early Cobras. During some racing events, it was found necessary to flare out front and rear fenders both to clear the tires and meet competition specifications that fenders extend as far out as the hub. Fender flares have been increased to cover added rim width of all production cars and give clearance on the rear wheels. This additional valance flaring was obtained by enlarging diameter of the fender opening and moving the lip out to increase the radius, which gives the effect of a modified flare.

It was soon learned that the original cars without protection other than small vertical bumper guards couldn't help being battered in American parking lots. Underneath the Cobra skin there have been minor changes to uprights and bumper guard mountings to facilitate installation of Carroll Shelby's accessories. These are special bumpers, a grille guard in front and full width bumper across the rear. In the engine compartment are radiator brackets to support the new radiator and brackets for the engine mounting. Both are incorporated in production in England.

One thing that experienced Cobra drivers will notice is that current production cars show modifications to the brake, clutch pedal and throttle assembly. The throttle crank assembly was modified because Cobra mechanics found minor problems in pinning and maintaining the throttle linkage, which used to work loose from its shaft. Brake and clutch pedals show a little more offset to get more clearance between them. At the same time foot wells were increased in width to give more foot room for driver and passenger. Though this made clearance in the engine compartment more difficult, as far as exhaust pipe routing was concerned, it has resulted in a more comfortable arrangement for the driver.

Floor-mounted clutch and brake pedals were moved by bending the pivot arm. The pin or bolt pivot of each pedal is about three inches below the level of the Cobra floor. Push rods for brake and clutch hydraulic cylinders were about two inches above the pivot point, and the floor is above that. All bending, which modifies the pedals, is done above the floor. Pedals are mounted in a steel box and extend up through a rubber sealed plate to take up clearance and prevent entry of cold air from outside. Early Cobras had inadequate room in the driver's compartment for a tall person. Soon A.C. Cars was modifying Cobras in production to gain more space. A repositioning of instruments put them in a more convenient area for driver viewing. When Cobras began coming through with rack and pinion steering, the space problem was solved. The car steered so much lighter, Shelby eliminated the adjustable steering column which few drivers ever used. By eliminating this feature they were able to add an inch or so of arm room in the car. As one Cobra mechanic told us, "That new rack and pinion really makes a helluva nice car compared to the old one with worm and sector. There's just a world of difference."

All production Cobras, since late 1963, utilize American instruments, rather than the English-built units. Cobras went to the Ford alternator, Auto-Lite batteries and Stewart-Warner instruments with Ford transmitters. Many of these parts, including a wiring loom made in America, are shipped to England for installation in the Cobras by A.C. Cars Ltd. Only a small number of parts, such as the alternator and some of the lights are kept in America for installation at the Shelby American plant.

Basically, those parts that were difficult to install or assemble were shipped to England; those which could be added later without trouble were kept in the United States. Primary reason for this was to make it possible for all Shelby Cobra owners to have their cars serviced with parts available from any Ford dealer in the world. The previous mixture of Ford engine, with English electrical system and instruments, left much to be desired in the matter of obtaining simple and easy service.

A shipment of Cobras is received every week at the Shelby American plant in Venice, Cal. They arrive from the harbor on a large truck and are rolled off into the production shop. While cars have been arriving from England, transmissions have been arriving from Borg-Warner in Indiana. They are shipped on pallets in lots of 10 to 50. The Ford engines are

Prior to engine installation, all body work and touch up is completed. Large circle on trunk lid is where A.C. emblem has been removed.

Crated Ford Fairlane V-8 engines, in the foreground, are ready for "dress up" in which fan, alternator, transmission and other accessories are added.

received completely crated, minus the generator, starter, fan belt, fan and water pump pulleys. All other accessories, referred to by Ford as "dress-up" items, are delivered to Shelby American by the same vendors who provide them to Ford Motor Company for regular production cars.

Transmissions used in the Cobra are worthy of note. They are production transmissions similar to that used in other Ford Motor products equipped with the four-speed stick shift in the center of the floor. An optional bell housing for the transmission is a special unit provided by Shelby American to contain the clutch should it shatter at the high speeds of competition. The standard clutch housing, main center casting and tail shaft housing are aluminum for lightness. Inside is a different set of gears than is used in the standard Ford iron-cased transmission, as well as a different spline on the input shaft. The Ford spline shaft is an inch and one eighth in diameter with ten splines. The spline in the Cobra transmission is an inch and a quarter in diameter with 12 splines. The Cobra box

The four-speed Ford-built transmission in Cobras is fully syncronized. All gears are in constant mesh, except the reverse sliding gear. Gear changes are made by sliding the toothed blocking ring in the direction of the numbered arrow.

57

has a set of Pontiac gears and shafts inside a Ford housing. As a result, on assembly, a Chevrolet clutch disc is matched with the Pontiac spline shaft inside the Shelby Cobra clutch housing.

To date there have been three different transmissions used in Cobras. The earliest was a four-speed Ford unit with an iron transmission case. This was the standard box used in other Ford production cars. First gear ratio was 2.36:1, Second had a ratio of 1.78:1 and Third was 1.41:1. The current "standard" transmission is the aluminum-cased Ford unit mentioned previously with the Pontiac gears. This gear set offers a better "split" of gears in which First is 2.20:1, Second 1.63:1 and Third is 1.31:1.

A third transmission, used only in the racing Cobras, is a totally different unit available as an option in 1964. This so-called "Sebring" transmission case is of aluminum. It has a First gear ratio of 2.33:1, Second gear of 1.61:1 and a Third gear of 1.20:1. By comparing ratios of the Sebring transmission it will be noticed that Third gear is a "long" gear which could well be used for almost anything near maximum speed. First gear is way down in the hole to give fantastic acceleration off the starting line, and out of Sebring's ten-mile-an-hour corner.

It's exciting to wander through the Shelby production plant. In one corner of the vast workroom is a selection of from ten to 30 engine-less A.C. Cobras. They are dirty, dusty, covered with the grime of shipping. They have no windshield though taillights are installed; a bumper is in back, there is Cosmaline all over the chrome and the tonneau cover is taped tightly in place over the cockpit. On the hood is taped an order indicating the ultimate owner of the car, its destination and every item of custom or optional equipment ordered with the specific unit.

Engine compartment wiring, from the loom, is loosely taped to chassis members with every wire carefully labeled to indicate its function and destination. Motor mounts, hood rod support and fan brackets are solidly welded and painted. In front, behind the radiator, is the tiny electric fan used in the Cobra to cool the radiator and save horsepower wasted by an engine-

"Cherry picker" supports engine while three men carefully guide it into location in the Cobra chassis.

mounted fan. Underneath the body fenders a complete job of undercoating has been done.

When a car gooes into production a team of skilled mechanics roll it into a work area. Here pre-modification begins. The hood is removed and hooked onto a special hanger on the wall where it is secure and safe from possible damage while the engine is being installed. A kit of "goodies" is ready to be fitted to the car. The battery is installed, grille fitted, the floor modified for special shift linkage, throttle stops matched, a steel line fitted for the hydraulic clutch, windshield wipers mounted, the gas line clamped to the frame at several points along its full length, water and oil temperature lines installed, starter solenoid mounted, and a number of other minor modifications completed before the car is ready to move to the buildup line.

Meanwhile, on one of the six engine-buildup stands, a new Ford 289-V8 has been mounted. The clutch housing and clutch have been removed, the Chevrolet clutch plate installed to match the Borg-Warner T-10 transmission (with Pontiac gears) and a new clutch housing fitted. The standard Ford thermostat has been removed and a new one, of 160°F opening, has

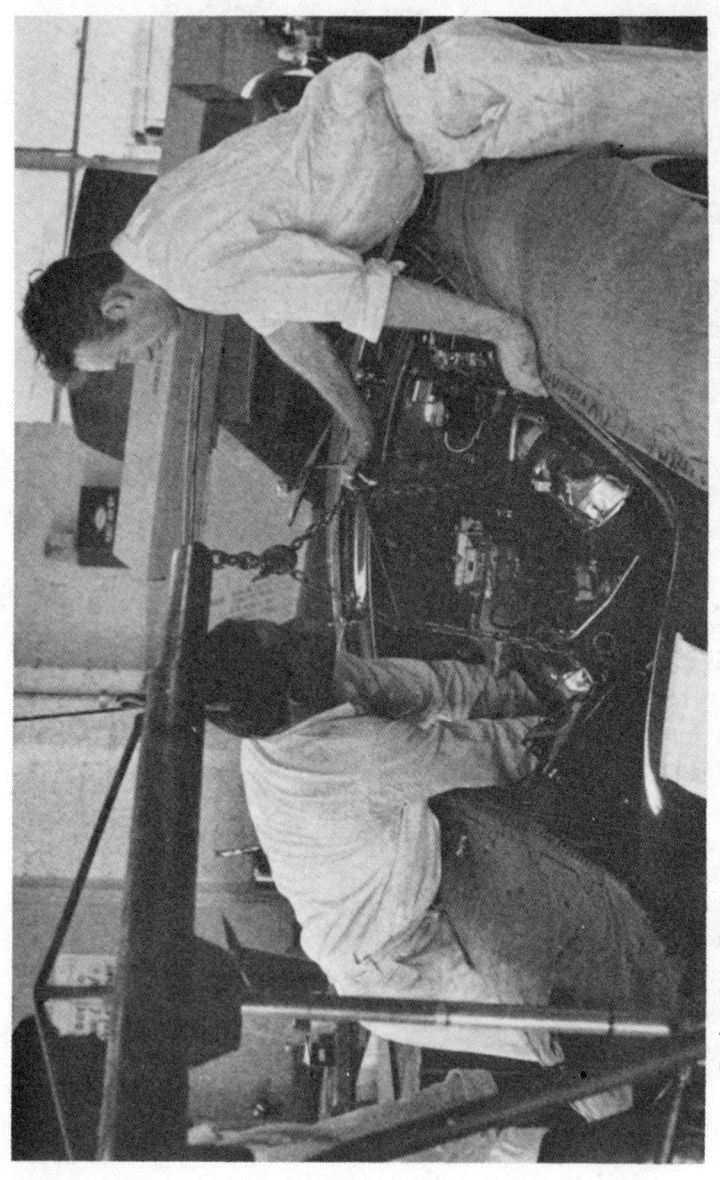

Engine installation is begun with the power plant supported by a small "Cherry picker." Production orders are taped to the front of each Cobra. After each operation the mechanic must sign off his work. Producion records on every Cobra detail each phase of the custom-quality build-up.

been fitted. Shelby Cobra valve covers replace plain steel covers on the heads, the air cleaner has been installed, plus alternater, crankshaft pulley, starter and other minor dress-up items. Each of these V-8 engines from Ford is inspected and run-in. Tolerances are close on them and each one is as near to a custom-built engine as is possible to have in this day of mechanized production.

On the engine dress-up a small Falcon six-cylinder fan is put on the pulley. Cobra buyers are advised to leave it on for four to five thousand miles while the engine undergoes its break-in. This eliminates the possibility of over-heating and subsequent engine damage. At the end of 5,000 miles it can be removed and reliance placed on the small electric fan to cool the engine. However, Shelby American specialists have found that in hot areas of the southern U. S., it is better to leave the fan on. The fabulous torque and power of the Fairlane V-8 is more than adequate for the Cobra. The small fan takes such a minor amount of horsepoower that it is hardly noticeable to the average driver.

The now completed modified A.C. Cobra chassis has been pushed up onto one of six roll-on stands. These stands, about 16 inches above the floor, are where each car is completely assembled. There are two men and one car to each stand.

There is no "production line" at Shelby American. Each car is mounted on a seperate stand. Here, skilled mechanics completely build a car, assuming responsibility for each operation.

61

Limited production schedules of Shelby American allow custom building of each Cobra. Mechanics follow a single car through to completion.

These skilled mechanics are completely responsible for the car's performance. Assisting and guiding them is a leadman who provides advice and acts as a working foreman. Once a car is on the stand, the complete engine is hoisted over and installed in place. About forty hours of work are required to turn a stripped chassis from the storage area into a shining and brilliant performing Cobra. By mid-1964, the Shelby firm was turning out three to four cars a day.

Unique in automobile assembly plants is the Cobra final inspection sheet. On it are seventy-five different operations considered necessary for shipping approval. Each car is driven over one of two routes and each is run-in at 1500 RPM in an open area of the assembly division. It's then test driven about 30 miles and given a complete final inspection for mechanical perfection.

At this time, body trim is brought to concourse condition. Metal work is repaired, primed and then painted to the highest standards of custom craftsmanship. Once the paint is set, the entire car is polished and detailed for delivery. Either Leon-

Each car is polished and detailed to concourse condition prior to delivery.

ard Parsons, production supervisor, or his shop foreman personally test each car after which it is delivered to the Shelby American sales department for shipment to the ultimate customer.

Even production specialists have played a part in modifying Cobras to meet American standards of comfort. Parsons learned that a number of customers complained about difficulty of operating the clutch. (Shelby American test drivers had handled so many sports cars they didn't notice the clutch was heavy.) There were a number of ways this could be improved. One was to use a different size hydraulic cylinder; another to modify the length of the clutch throw lever. Parsons spent a week and a half working with the problem. He soon found that by drilling a mounting hole a half inch down from the original location of the clutch cylinder push rod attachment that the clutch would function properly but require much less pressure. As a result, production Cobras have a clutch that is nearly as light as any of Dearborn's passenger cars. But it is sufficiently solid to allow rear wheels to burn rubber at almost any speed up to and including well over 100 miles an hour.

Pete Brock (left) is designer of the Daytona Cobra coupe, shown here in mockup form. The wooden frame was built on a standard Cobra chassis.

Side view of Daytona Cobra shows manner in which mockup was built on Cobra chassis.

Impressive reduction in height was made in basic design of Daytona Cobra by lowering the seating position. Carroll Shelby, in the roadster, checks out seating position of Cobra driver Ken Miles.

For the future, there is the Cobra GT coupe, one of the most unique vehicles built in the United States. It's based on the standard Cobra chassis. With modest horsepower increases (about 380 horsepower) from the 289-cubic-inch engine, Cobra designer Pete Brock figures the new coupe will be good for about 200 miles an hour. If additional speed is needed, to beat the Ferraris at their own game (long distance racing) there is a good chance that the 427-cubic-inch V-8 could be installed. It will have a complete belly pan which is expected to add 15 to 20 miles an hour top speed. The car, termed "real slippery looking", has a frontal area much less than the Cobra.

Whether it turns out to be the Cobra of the future, only time will tell. A number of Cobra designs are causing extensive activity on the drawing board, in dynamometer rooms and wind tunnels throughout the world.

4. Production Cobras on the Street

For this Cobra book, Englishman Ken Miles, one of the leading sports car drivers, gave us his views on driving a Cobra for maximum fun.

Miles' racing experience dates back to early 1950 when he was campaigning on the Pacific Coast with a small combination of Morris Minor parts and MG performance equipment known as the "Flying Shingle". This home built collection of bits and pices, of Miles' design, literally wiped up small bore competition as long as Ken chose to drive it. Since then he's successfully driven almost every production racing machine seen in the U.S. His greatest victories have been with the Porsche, variations of the MG and currently with Shelby's Cobra. Here, in an exclusive interview for Sports Car Press, are Ken's candid comments on driving the street version of the Cobra.

*** * * ****

"Ken, what would you suggest a Cobra buyer do to gain experience and confidence in handling his car on the street? Is there any special procedure he should go through?"

"No. The car is just as easy to drive as any other car except it has a little bit more power. I don't know of any unusual technique that is required to get experience. If a fellow can drive at all, he can drive a Cobra. There's just no trick to driving the Cobra."

"How would you describe a Cobra, Ken?"

"The street model Cobra is a fairly docile machine. It's like a big strong MG which has more speed, a solid stick shift gear box, rather quick rack and pinion steering, and exceedingly good brakes. It is a small, very maneuverable, car. A Cobra doesn't require any particular skill to drive providing you use a certain amount of preparedness. It gets going so quickly, so soon, that you can get involved in difficulty before you realize it unless you keep in mind that it's a real power-house. In the Cobra you have a car with far better acceleration than any comparable-size sports car on the market and sometimes we're a bit inclined to underestimate it. You can arrive at the next red light a little before you expect to and once brakes stop the wheels from going around, they serve no further useful purpose.

"Discretion is the watchword. Other than that, there's no trick to it at all. It's a docile and perfectly road-worthy machine. New drivers find its steering is rather unusual in that you can put into a corner quite fast. You always have enough power so that if you get into trouble you can give it a bit more throttle and bring the back end around. Away you go. On the other hand, if you panic and back off the throttle, it won't do anything like swap ends. It's a very easy car to drive."

"Would your technique of driving this car be different from that of driving a European roadster?"

"Terribly different, of course. You don't need to change gears all the time in a Cobra. If you want to pass something you just stomp on the throttle. There's no need to take another gear unless you're in an awful hurry. Fourth will get you by almost anything quickly. If you're driving a hundred miles an hour on the road and want to pass something in a hurry, it will get up and go. Don't worry about shifting. Just punch it and point it."

"Let's assume you're sitting at the corner with the engine running. What are your suggestions for coordinating clutch and throttle when making the initial start in first gear?"

"I try to handle a street car the same as I do a racing car. That is, get the clutch fully engaged at the lowest possible engine revs without stalling the engine. Actually the clutch in this car is extremely robust and will take all sorts of punishment. Of course the less throttle you have when you engage the clutch, the less loading you put on the transmission, the final drive, tires, wheel spokes is the best throttle. The car just lasts longer that way."

"Is clutch action progressive or rather sudden?"

"It's quite progressive though the clutch pedal is fairly heavy because we have such a big engine. The pedal has to be pushed pretty much all the way down before the clutch will release. When you let the clutch out, it engages over a fairly long travel so there's no excuse for stalling the engine. There's plenty of feel that the clutch is engaged long before it's all the way home. You can always get off the line without stalling the engine. I find that when I take off on idle, I don't bother to open the throttle. I just let the clutch in gently. When it's fully engaged, I open the throttle. The Cobra engine has fantastic low-speed torque and with the idle settled down at about five or six hundred revs, it will pull you off the mark quite happily without any throttle at all."

"What about shifting from first to second gear?"

"As far as driving on the street is concerned, as soon as the Cobra's under way, I drop into second gear; probably not doing more than fifteen miles an hour. If you give a car a lot of throttle in low gear you only spin the wheels anyway. The real objective is to get out of first gear as soon as you can. You're not going anywhere until you get into second. In fact, I like to get into third gear as soon as possible because the engine doesn't need to be reving to produce an awful lot of power. If you are really on the run, and want to get out and shake somebody up, you can take it up to 6500 revs in any gear and really get moving."

"In other words, for maximum acceleration on the street model, you'd let it idle out in first then shift to second. How fast would you run it out in second Ken?"

"I'd run it up to about 6000 revs."

"Then do you run another 6000 in third?"

"Yes. A Cobra shifts out, and accelerates best, at very high speed. I think on the production model this (6000 rmp) represents around 90 to 100 miles an hour or perhaps a little more than that."

"In shifting while the car is moving, do you pop your clutch about halfway or do you have to disengage fully?"

"You have to disengage it fully unless you're awfully careful with the gear shift lever. If you don't disengage it all the way, what happens is that you can't override the synchromesh. The Ford synchro is absolutely unbeatable. If you don't put your clutch down all the way, it simply won't go into gear."

"Do you have to manhandle the gear shift lever or can you just slap it with your palm from gear to gear?"

"You can put it across and shift with a touch. It's an extremely light, very nice shift provided you do one of two things. Either push the clutch down all the way or get your shift timing absolutely precise. The engine has a very light flywheel so it rises and falls very rapidly. It's difficult to catch it at exactly the right moment, so it's must easier to push the clutch all the way down, so it's completely free, then make your shift."

"What is your opinion of driving a Cobra at low speed, in fourth gear, on the street?"

"Well, provided the thing isn't running so slow that it's bucking and hammering at the transmission, it really doesn't matter how slow you drive it. The engine is so docile, and in such a mild state of tune, that you're not going to hurt it at all by lugging it. Of course, if you lug to the point where the transmission is chattering, you're damaging your transmission, driveline and rear end. But you've got to be down pretty slow before that happens. You'll find that you can come down to about 30 miles an hour in high gear, stomp on the throttle and take off. You won't hurt anything—least of all the engine."

"Regarding use of automatic transmissions, what are your thoughts on driving, Ken?"

"One of the things that makes it fun to drive, for a racing man like myself who has changed enough gears to last a lifetime, is to have an automatic transmission on a sports car. There's two pedals. One says 'Let's Go' and the other says 'Stop.' You just take your choice and push it."

"What is the difference in handling and cornering when a car is equipped with an automatic transmission?"

"For extremely fast driving, I don't like an automatic transmission. You can't come up to a corner and get into the next lower gear and be all set to power out of it. You have to approach the corner on dead throttle; then, when you get around, stop so it will shift down and you can take off. This is irritating. It's also much slower than approaching a corner with a manual transmission in the proper gear."

"Why is it slower, Ken?"

"Because (with an automatic) you have a point in time when you don't have control over the car. When you're approaching a corner in the normal manner, in a stick shift car, you're already in gear braking down to whatever speed you find necessary to make your next shift. Now at this point you haven't entered the turn. As you enter the turn, with the car on part throttle, you can steer the car with the throttle. If you find you're going a little bit too hard, you can ease off the throttle and the engine will act as a brake. It's a very effective brake because you're in a lower gear.

"Or you can open the throttle a little bit and kick the back end out if you want to make like a race driver. Then you come out of the turn starting to open the throttle more smoothly. As the Cobra leaves the turn you progressively steer more and more out of the turn into a straight line. You can give the car more and more throttle smoothly without wheel spin or any sudden jerk. Competition driving with an automatic will find you going into the corner on dead throttle in high gear. You start out of the corner and just at the point where you least want to disturb the transmission, and you're trying to achieve a fine balance between torque on rear wheels and attitude of the car, the bloody thing changes gear. Then you don't know what to do."

"How would you suggest Cobra drivers corner if their car is equipped with an automatic transmission?"

"Drive much slower. In the first place, they just have to go more slowly with an automatic shift car in driving of that type.

If you had overriding controls so you could persuade the thing to shift down at any time into the next lower gear, this would be fine, but you don't."

"*I understand that there are some automatic transmissions which do have overriding controls.*"

"There's really no satisfactory box available in the United States. Those we have don't seem to be very good. Hot rodders have some reworked American transmissions but I have no experience with those. The English have an excellent one in the Hobbs which has this overriding feature. It's a very, very good box indeed and the driver has complete control over all the shifts. They have a great advantage over the stick shift with this transmission in that the driver knows what gear he's in when he wants it in that gear. You don't have this sudden change of torque loading on the tires which can be so embarrassing to play with."

"*About cornering by using your throttle—how does the driver of a street car tell when he's in need of more or less throttle while cornering on pavement.*"

"Two things should tell him whether he needs more or less throttle. One is common sense. If he knows he's going too fast, he'd better get off of it or he's going to run into something.

"Of course you might arrive at a situation where the car is in an understeering condition and rapidly heading off the road on the outside of the turn. It's a case of great rarity, much rarer than people like to believe, when you can save this situation by deliberate application of throttle. Added throttle may cause the back end to swing out and reposition the car, changing its attitude so that side thrust from the rear wheels will help to go around the corner instead of helping it go straight off the road. When to do this is something that you just learn by experience.

"Of course, if the car is pointing the wrong way, turning the steering wheel isn't going to do a thing for you except increase the already existing understeer condition. Your only hope is to get the back end around to improve the attitude of the car through the corner. When you give it more throttle you have to realize that in doing so, you're going to increase your speed. This certainly isn't an infallible cure to the situation where you've gone into a corner too fast.

"Frankly if you go into the corner too fast, you're in trouble with any car under any circumstances and should realize that this added throttle is not always the answer to the situation. You do occasionally find yourself in a mess. Then you have to decide which end of the motor car you're going to bend. Since the back end is further away from me, sitting in front, I usually like to bend the back. You must give the car a little more throttle than the tires will stand and sometimes this will resolve the situation so the car will be pointing down the road out of the corner."

"What are situations where you'd say it would be a good idea to get your foot off the throttle in a big fat hurry?"

"You could be in a situation where you're not going terribly fast or, with some cars, in a situation where you're going very fast and the car is going straight on instead of going around a corner. Under certain circumstances you can ease off the throttle and reduce thrust on the front wheels. This will enable the front tires to get a better bite and pull you fully around the corner. This is particularly true of a car that is inherently a very understeering car. The tires in this situation are acting as somewhat of a brake. They are not pointing directly around the corner. They are really pointing at a greater angle than you are actually turning. The car and weight of the engine is generating a sideways force which is away from the direction the tire is turning. Any reduction of this thrust by the engine and car weight will result in a reduction of the sideways force so that available traction capacity of the tire is more usefully applied in pulling you around the corner.

"We consider a tire to always have a certain available capacity for transmitting steering loads. Any part of that capacity which you absorb, by pushing it sideways with the engine or using its brake, is force which is not available for cornering. This is the basic reason that you would not normally apply brakes in a corner. When you're part way around the corner, tires are already generating the maximum possible cornering force on the car to pull it around. If you apply the brakes you're going to reduce available traction for cornering (turning) which is going to give the car a very strong tendency to go straight ahead. The same thing applies if the car is going to corner on a good deal of dirt. Ease off on the throttle and you'll sometimes decrease the side thrust load on the tire which gives you a better chance of getting around the corner.

"Under competition conditions, where you're going into the corner with a lot of throttle, you're arriving in a grossly oversteering condition where the tail of the car is beginning to hang out badly. Under those circumstances your only hope of salvation is to ease off the throttle. Capacity of rear tires for holding the car on the road has now been exceeded. If the rear end of the car is out, because you're imposing so much driving load on the tires from the engine, you're using all their capacity to drive the car which leaves not very much to steer it. In order to get the back tires to grip the road again and straighten you up, you have to reduce the driving load. This you do by backing off on the throttle. Since the tires are not now transmitting as much power to the road as they were before, you have more traction available to steer the car.

"Situations under which you back off the throttle for oversteer, won't have you backing off the throttle if in an understeering condition. This is something you can only learn from experience. Perhaps a particular car at X miles an hour, in X radius turn, at such and such a camber, and such and such a car's frictional relationship to the road, would be driven in this manner; whereas the actual number of combinations and circumstances are so infinite there's just no way to decide without experience. You can't drive a car on paper."

"Ken, what is your opinion of the steering wheel position in a street model Cobra?"

"It suits me fairly well. It's far away and upright. The seating position of the car is quite good. Even for a tall man like myself, there's room in the car. It's a tremendously roomy car but then, it's rather small too."

After A.C. Cars purchased production rights to the chassis design, Tojeiro built a "one-off" sports car with Jaguar engine.

"What about the diameter of the wheel? Do you have any leverage assist from it?"

"Enough. Steering is quite light. There's a good deal of kick-back from road shock which is inevitable when you get very light in the steering. Any big car with rack and pinion steering is going to give you a certain amount of reaction to wheel problems and potholes. This is inevitable if you want sensible and accurate control."

"Does this kick-back change the position of the wheel in your hand or does it change direction of the car?"

"It only changes the wheel position in your hand. It doesn't affect the direction in which the car is pointing. It isn't irritating. I mention it because the driver of the average American sedan holds his steering wheel like it's connected to a pot of porridge. The steering wheel of most American cars swings quite widely without affecting direction of the car."

"You mentioned that the steering is rather quick, Ken. What about understeering and oversteering?"

"The Cobra's got a certain amount of inherent understeering which can be very quickly transformed into an oversteering condition by use of torque and throttle. Any certain jab of acceleration is going to give you gobs of oversteer which results naturally because weight distribution on the car is close to 50-50. You only have about a thousand pounds of weight on the rear wheels and when you use the sort of torque a Ford V-8 puts out, you go around awfully easily."

"Is there any particular technique of handling this car in traffic driving?"

"Aim the car and open the throttle."

"Are the Cobra brakes exceedingly good?"

"Yes. They are powered though really there's no need for power systems on such a light car. The Girling (made in England) disc brakes are generously sized to put it mildly. For 1964 we have an even larger brake than we had before and a differential caliper system which gives us more pad area, longer life and better braking."

"Did the revised braking system make any difference to pedal pressure?"

"It's just a little lighter and requires a little less pedal pressure. The pedal pressure in any disc brake system is fairly high unless you use a booster. Those on the Cobra are just about the same pressure requirements as needed for a passenger car with fairly hard lining."

"Do Cobra brakes come on all at once?"

"No, they're fairly progressive and very easy indeed."

"Are there any undesirable characteristics in the Cobra when you use the brakes in a corner?"

"Generally speaking, it's never desirable to brake in a corner. You do of course in competition and you may do it on the street a little bit. When you're entering a slow curve and want to generally reduce speed you can apply them quite hard provided you don't use them to the point where you lose contact with the road. The car will maintain its attitude and continue just the way it's pointing. A Cobra is extremely useful in that respect. It does not become affected by use of moderate throttle openings or heavy braking. However violent throttle opening will produce wheel spin, and things like that, which end up reducing tire adhesion with the road."

"What's the maximum speed at which you can lock up brakes on a street model Cobra?"

"We're using the same brakes on our racing cars that we use on the street version. You can lock the wheels going 160 miles an hour."

"Ken, are there any hints that you'd like to pass on about using brakes during bad weather while driving the street model?"

"The same approach would suit the Cobra as applies to any car you're driving in wet weather. You're faced with a situation where you don't have as good coefficient of friction between the tire and roads as you do in dry weather. You have to allow yourself more room to stop. This applies to Lincolns, Fords and Cobras. You do have an advantage with disc brakes in that connection because they are completely insensitive to rain. You'll never lose brakes on the highway or the corner because the disc brakes has an inherent self cleaning action in which the first rotation of the wheel cleans the disc."

"Ken, do you think the street version of the Cobra would be ideal for a woman to use shopping?"

"No."

"Do you think the average woman would enjoy driving it?"

"Certainly. It's a lot of fun to drive. It's a nice light car and has lots of power. It's really an enjoyable car to drive. You asked if it was a suitable car to go shopping in and I said the answer was 'No'. I wouldn't consider any big car as proper to go shopping in. I'd buy one of those little 'tiddlers', like a mini-Minor or Volkswagen or MG or something like that. I can't see the point in taking two tons of machinery, 400 horsepower and using several gallons of gas to zip down to the market and back. My family lives up in the Hollywood Hills and I drive a Ford station wagon. When I use my wagon to drive to the market, I get about 2000 miles on a set of tires. I can do the same driving in a smaller car and do it quicker and more conveniently. Besides using a great deal less gas and getting 10,000 miles on a set of tires.

"Of course, if I'm going to the theatre, or going up to Santa Barbara for a weekend race or to Mexico City, I like the big car. But when I'm going away somewhere for the weekend by myself or with my wife and without the family, I think the Cobra is marvelous. There's all sorts of power and it's a lot of fun to drive on the highway. It makes it a real pleasure to leave the freeways and turnpikes and take more circuitous routes to enjoy the pleasure of handling a sports car that drives as though it were on rails."

Cobra driver Ken Miles, one of the finest sports car driver/engineers in the United States.

5. Building Racing Cobras

The Shelby Cobra was an almost instant success on American race tracks. The trophy gathering resulted from skilled drivers supported by mechanics who had the knowledge and equipment to maintain the finest racing vehicle that had hit sports car tracks in many years.

In initial phases of the Cobra racing program, a production car was stripped and modified into a racing machine. Today the English A.C. factory builds a "production" car that includes many of these "performance" modifications. But for the benefit of all sports car owners and drivers of older unmodified Cobras, we explain modifications the Shelby American people made in their cars to insure safety for the drivers and a place in the winner's circle.

In effect, they start with a bare frame and pile of parts. First to go is one of the two windshield wipers since sports car regulations require only one. A second simple modification is removal of the standard horns. Reason for this is that horns on the production Cobra are quite bulky. They fit ahead of the radiator, in the air duct, cutting down flow of cooling air, and they weigh about 12 pounds. Racing mechanics install a small French horn weighing about 1½ pounds. This saving, of over ten pounds, is only one step in the all-important weight reduction needed to change a street-model Cobra into a race winner.

While the frame is bare, the forward socket for the roll bar, is welded to a frame cross member on the right side of the transmission just forward of the passenger seat. Two additional sockets are welded to a frame cross-member behind the driver's seat. The bars, of 3/16" wall, chromalloy steel tubing an inch and a quarter in diameter, slip down over these sockets. Aircraft-type bolts fasten through the socket and roll bar tube to hold them together. The roll bar comes up in an inverted "U" behind the driver's body and there is a diagonal brace angling downward, on the driver's right, through the passenger compartment. It locks into the third socket welded to the frame to the right of the transmission and bars become, in effect, extensions of the Cobra chassis frame.

When the installation is complete mechanics make a simple but definitive test. Using a chain fall, they lift the car by the roll bar and sway it back and forth. Though the roll bar is off center, and the car hangs at an angle, the bar proves its stiffness and strength. In racing, more than one Cobra has been stood on its head without damage to the carefully engineered and installed roll bar or driver.

Special seat belt brackets are welded to frame cross members behind the driver. Two forged eyebolts, screwed into the frame brackets, are fitted with swivels and clips. The clip-type racing seat belt is hooked to the eyebolts while the shoulder harness is matched to the shape of the roll bar U-member behind the driver's shoulders.

Another alteration to the racing Cobras is installation of a rheostat for the dashlight. With it a driver can dim the dashlight to suit his convenience during nighttime racing. At the same time a fuel pressure gauge is installed in the instrument panel. Drivers find this one of their more valuable instruments. If the engine begins to falter a quick glance at the fuel pressure gauge will indicate whether the problem is electrical, mechanical or fuel.

Two modifications involve the left door. Many fine racing drivers have such long arms that there was not sufficient elbow room for them to swing the wheel in a hurry. The simple answer is a reduction in height of the left door where it curves near the steering wheel to provide additional elbow room. A second door change is a cover over the left door hinge. Cobra drivers found that on hard, long races, where they were being thrown about inside the car, the left leg became sore from repeated contact with the door hinge. Shelby American mechanics cover it with a metal plate and a thick layer of sponge rubber and the driver now has something to brace his leg against on corners.

A small CO_2 or other approved fire extinguisher is mounted on the transmission tunnel between the seats. Though some racing associations do not require its installation, all Shelby American racing Cobras carry the fire extinguisher. They wear a bullet-type mirror, usually mounted conventionally in the middle of the dash panel. Occasionally a driver has one on either side of one door or the other. Some drivers like to in the middle of the dashboard and one on each door.

Another driver-inspired modification involves construction and location of control pedals. Brakes, clutch and throttle pedals on production cars are of cast alloy. Many race drivers have such a heavy foot they can break these off in the heat of serious competition. Shelby American makes new pedals, of steel. The throttle pedal modification includes a travel stop limiting movement of the pedal. Drivers in their eagerness to win do not stop to think, "Go easy, this is the throttle." They just put the foot down until it stops and in many cases the travel stop, underneath the aluminum pedal, would break the casting when the driver stomped on his car in a hurry. A new throttle pedal of steel corrects this situation and allows modification of pedal size to suit driver convenience.

Frequently, throttle pedal location is changed to suit different drivers. Cobra mechanics can modify the height of the throttle pad in relation to brake, clutch and floor pan. It can be offset nearly an inch in either direction to suit the individual. This is done by bending the stem of the pedal after it is heated. Because the pedal has a fixed socket, it can rise at an angle to left or right, depending on a driver's personal preference. Modification of throttle linkage includes replacing assembly screws with bolts and self-locking nuts to eliminate any possible loosening. This is done for the throttle housing tube which fits on top of the foot box. On early cars the clutch pedal linkage ratio, in relation to the clutch master cylinder, was such that drivers were troubled with excessive pressure in the hydraulic system while releasing the clutch. This ratio was changed by an alteration in connection between master cylinder rod and clutch pedal. Shortly after the modification was proven successful, plans were sent to England and all A.C. cars now include this change. The hydraulic line connection between clutch cylinder and slave at the clutch housing is a section of copper tubing containing an anti-vibration coil. On racing Cobras a flexible metal hose is installed that works with the engine as it twists and torques. To support the hose metal clips are welded onto the frame. From the flex hose connection, a steel tube leads to the clutch master cylinder attached to the cowl. In this installation, the flex line between frame and clutch can move, while the steel tube between frame connection and master cylinder insures that leakage accidents will not take place.

As a safety factor, double brake fluid reservoir tanks are installed on the cowl. Should there be a slight leak in the hydraulic system the Cobra driver has ample fluid to handle the leak until it can be repaired. This does not change the number of master cylinders but merely doubles capacity of brake fluid reserve.

Special fuel lines and reserve system are installed in every racing Cobra. Aircraft-type armored tube 3/8" I.D., has proven safe and ample for maximum fuel flow. There are two lines, one from the reserve and one from the main source of supply. The reserve is a two-to-three gallon standpipe in the bottom of the fuel tank. A three-way valve is installed where the driver can reach it conveniently. In a close, race when the driver is working on time, and doesn't want to make a fuel stop, he can run on his main tank until it is out of fuel. Then he has the two-to-three gallon cushion and can come in for his fuel stop at the most opportune time. This is a safety factor and can help win races by allowing the driver to exercise judgment as to the amount of fuel he will end the race with.

The competition fuel tank, of 37-gallon capacity, replaces a standard 14-gallon tank found in street Cobra. A Bendix or Stewart-Warner electric fuel pump is mounted below the tank on a rear suspension member. From this position it pressurizes the entire fuel system and primes the carburetors before the engine is started. The mechanical fuel pump on the Ford V-8 engine remains in the system and acts as a measuring device to provide the proper amount of fuel in relation to engine speed. The new racing fuel tank has fuel feed lines to the electric pump leading down through the bottom of the trunk well, rather close to the spare tire. Accordingly, a special bracket is fabricated to keep the spare tire from hitting the tank outlet lines and breaking them off, since in competition a spare tire is frequently thrown in and out of a tank with great speed.

It was found that at high speeds, air flow over the back of the car would sometimes suck gasoline out of the filter tube through the vent opening and mist it over the driver. To prevent this, a baffle, somewhat like a half-moon section of metal, is fitted on the rear deck between the driver and tank filler neck. It's little more than a raised ledge on the body between the filler tube and the cockpit opening, but it breaks up air flow around the filler tank neck to eliminate the suction. Also, when the driver remains in the car during refueling, it prevents excess fuel from spilling into the cockpit. Overflow gasoline, instead of dripping into the cockpit, is caught by the baffle and drained off toward the rear of the car.

A final installation at the rear of the car includes modifications to the trunk lid latch. The basic production Cobra trunk has space for the spare tire, tools and luggage. The body of the car is quite low and on racing turns, or bumps and thumps of competition, it could twist enough to release the trunk latch. Shelby American mechanics install a pin in the trunk lid and two separate pins low down on the body of the car. An elastic hold-down strap with a loop at each end holds the trunk lid to the body, yet can be instantly relaxed when it is necessary to reach the spare tire or fuel tank.

At the other end of the racing Cobra, modifications are made to the hood. Latches are wing nuts which make it extremely simple to open in a hurry without use of a key or wrench. A modification includes use of spring-type sockets so that when the butterfly nut is turned home, the hood is down to stay. These aircraft-type latches (known as Dzus fasteners) are frequently found on light planes to hold cowling and inspection plates in place.

In early competition events Shelby American mechanics found that at high speed, air pressure in the engine compartment was so great, portions of the hood frame tended to lift. They now "pop-rivet" sections of the hood, and surrounding sheet metal, to make sure this cannot happen. The additional pop-rivets also eliminate possibility of sheet metal loosening should the Cobra driver shunt another car. During early races the hood support rod would occasionally vibrate loose and rattle around inside the engine compartment. A modification here includes use of a positive type catch that clips, locks and holds the rod in place. At the same time the catch can be instantly released, so the hood rod can be put to use in a hurry, when necessary.

The top of the hood has a hole cut in it for an air scoop which is pop-riveted over the hole. This scoop, rising slightly above the hood level, will catch cold air and direct it toward the carburetors. As a part of this installation an air box is built which fits over the carburetors. This box matches the air scoop in the hood so that when the hood is down the air scoop is directing cold, clean air directly into the carburetor. In this way, none of the hot air from the radiator, which is inside the engine compartment, can reach the carburetors and reduce maximum power output of the engine.

During early racing efforts of the Cobra, Shelby American mechanics were doing everything possible to save weight. They removed one of the two 4-inch air ducts leading from in front of the radiator, on each side of the core opening, up past the wheel, through the wheel well and down into the foot wells. But they soon found that the tremendous power of the Ford

Fairlane V-8 made this weight-saving gesture unnecessary, and drivers complained of the cockpit being too hot. Both ducts are now left in all production racing cars since their comfort-value is high.

The radiator comes in for a number of racing modifications, none of which are necessary for the street version of the car. (It is interesting to note that Shelby mechanics run the same 13-lb. pressure cap on the race car as on the street car.) One change for racing is offset-mounting a steel header tank on top of the front spring perch. Aluminum radiator baffles, made of sheet stock, are fitted around the front of the radiator to funnel all in-coming air toward the radiator. The baffles make sure none of the air entering the body opening can go between the radiator and body but must pass through the core to provide maximum cooling.

A novel radiator modification is installation of a "shaker" screen—a piece of heavy wire mesh hung in front of the radiator, mounted up under the body on four springs. It catches rocks and reavy debris that come in through the front air ducts, and the springs allow it to vibrate and shake off anything that might stick and reduce air flow to the radiator core.

Though rubber radiator hose has proven quite satisfactory on Cobra street models, it has been found inadequate for racing. Shelby American mechanics form steel pipe to go between the engine block and the radiator. Short lengths of rubber hose connect the block with the steel pipe, and the steel pipe with the radiator. In addition to this, black plastic electrical tape is used to wrap the rubber vibration hose to stiffen the hose while protecting it from possible damage of flying rocks or parts from other cars. As a result, almost every water connection of the engine cooling system is metal or short sections of rubber reinforced and protected with several layers of tightly wrapped tape.

All ordinary bolts are replaced by aircraft-quality nuts and bolts. In one situation at Sebring, when Dan Gurney was doing extremely well, on a sharp corner, he left the course. Coming back, the impact of front wheels hitting a curb sheared machine screws holding the rack and pinion assembly to the frame. His pit stop took an hour and forty minutes. Shelby American mechanics feel they lost this race in the pit.

Because machine screws can be a weak point, they are now replaced with standard or oversize Army-Navy-type bolts with either self-locking or wired nuts. As a part of this safety program, Allen screws holding caps on the lower front suspension ball joints are drilled and wired to make sure they won't come loose during competition.

One of the lessons learned in early Cobra racing was that when you drill a lubrication hole in a bolt you decrease its strength. This was discovered when a suspension-arm hanger pivot bolt broke during competition. Now, Shelby American mechanics manufacture hanger bolts for both front and rear suspension minus lubrication holes for fittings. After every race all such suspension hanger bolts are removed, inspected and lubricated by hand before replacement. A special low-friction silicone lubricant, is used and Shelby American mechanics say they have never had any problems from lack of lubrication during competition, nor have they ever lost a race due to failure of one of their solid suspension pivot members.

As is well known, the racing Cobras use wide-base magnesium wheels. Such wheels are necessary to get sufficient rubber on the ground to handle a Cobra's tremendous acceleration and braking potential. The wide-base rims interfere somewhat with steering arms and steering rods from the rack and pinion steering assembly of a street-model Cobra. Accordingly, the steering arm is removed, heated, put in a press, and bent to provide adequate clearance. After it has been reset, each steering arm is ground and inspected for surface cracks to make sure it has not faulted during the modification. The steering arm which comes from the kingpin position carries the steering rod on the front of the arm. The disc brake caliper is bolted to the rear of the arm.

Steering rods which project from ends of the rack-and-pinion steering box are shortened $3/4$" inch each. This total reduction of $1\frac{1}{2}$" is necessary for proper clearance from the magnesium wheels. At the same time the steering rod adjusting nuts are shortened to complete clearance modifications. According to drivers, this change of Cobra steering gives slightly more camber which shows up primarily when the wheels are in a bounce condition. Though the additional camber is said to make the car steer a bit harder, it does not disturb handling characteristics during a race as the additional camber is only a momentary condition when the wheels are in bounce.

Rear-wheel hub bearings are replaced with high-capacity ball bearings using a slightly larger ball in a wider bearing which fits into the hub carrier without additional machining. (Shelby American mechanics claim that running about 123 more horsepower than the standard engine, and the additional friction wear resulting from putting nearly twice the average tire on the road, warrants installation of the oversize bearings.) They are packed with a heavy-duty high-temperature grease to handle added power that the engine transmits to the ground. The combination of oversized bearings and special grease eliminates problems from friction building up into a heating problem in rear bearings.

Another problem, resulting from tremendous torque of the Ford V-8 engine, was a means of driving the rear wheels. It was found that splines in the magnesium wheels were not adequate to handle such extreme horsepower at competition speeds. Accordingly, bolts through the rear wheel hubs (which normally hold brake discs in place) are removed. They are replaced with six extremely hard, machined steel pins. These pins screw through the hubs and hold the discs on the hubs. The back of the disc has been counterbored so that a locknut can be fitted onto the threated end of the pin.

Halibrand magnesium wheels used on the Cobra have six drive holes in their central portion. These holes fit over the hardened steel drive pins and it is through these pins that the wheel is turned. In effect, the spline of the hub shaft, and knock-off nut, are little more than locating and holding fixtures. None of the drive torque is taken up by them.

As a part of the drive pin installation, both rear axle bearing carriers must be machined to clear lock nuts on the back of the brake disc. These are the same lock nuts that hold the drive pins in place. They fit so close, the rear bearing carrier must be machined to the contour of the hub so the lock nuts will clear the bearing cap.

Special racing exhaust headers installed on the Fairlane V-8 pass within three-quarters inch of the brake master cylinders; so close that the heat transfer has at times caused the brake and clutch fluid to boil. One of the more important innovations by Shelby American is to install a steel-asbestos shield to carry the heat away and prevent burns to mechanics' hands when they must fill the resevoirs in a hurry.

Custom brake pads (Corona, Class. BS-11) are installed in the Girling disc brake caliper. They are made of a hard compound of metallic and organic brake material mixture. Shelby American mechanics say they stand up well under heat and extreme wear.

Brake scoops are fabricated of aluminum sheet and pop-riveted onto the body and frame underneath the car in the air stream. They collect cold air and scoop it onto the brakes to cool the discs during competition racing.

On a few early racing Cobras, Shelby American mechanics had a problem with the leather differential front seal overheating and burning out. They built an air scoop and bolted it to the cross member just over the rear end. It projected into the air stream underneath the car and with a quarter turn directed air up onto the steel and over the rear end. Later neoprene seals which would hold up under extreme heat eliminated both the air scoop and loss of lubrication at the differential.

Differential overheating problems however, required more than a neoprene seal to solve. In long high speed races the powerful engine produced more torque than the three pints of oil in the differential could control. An oil cooler system was created by taking the engine oil cooler from a Sunbeam Alpine sports car and mounting it above the rear end, forward between the main frame members. The Sunbeam oil cooler is like a small-scale automobile radiator. Instead of

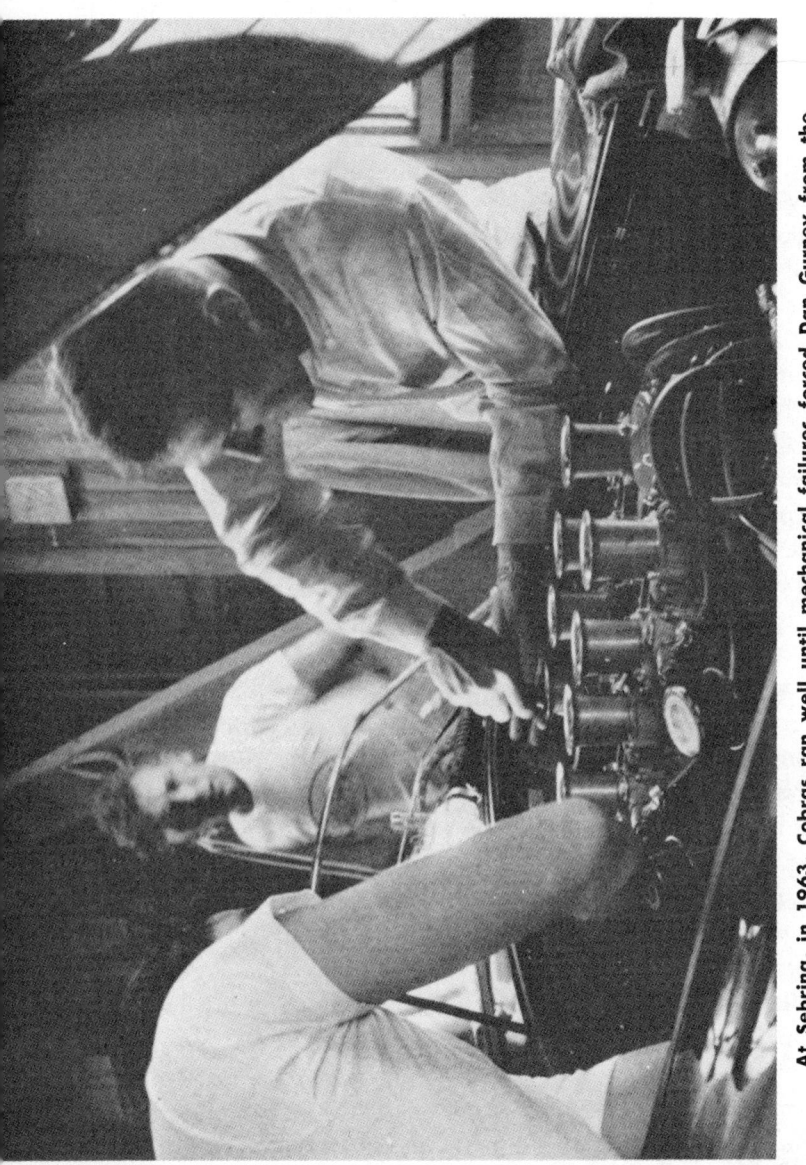

At Sebring, in 1963, Cobras ran well until mechanical failures forced Dan Gurney from the race. Another Cobra was plagued with brake problems. Facing the camera is Phil Remington. Aiding carburetor installation is Gurney. This Sebring Cobra had special transmission gears, Weber Carburetors and competition ignition system.

water, oil circulates while air is directed through the core to cool the oil via a small aluminum scoop projecting into the air stream. Pipe fittings were connected between the differential and oil cooler and a Bendix fuel pump in the system circulated the oil. An additional modification was installation of a larger breather tube of ½" pipe going all the way from the differential to the top of the roll bar to eliminate any pressure build-up inside the differential. By circulating three quarts of oil through the oil cooler, and relieving pressure build-up, Shelby American mechanics completely eliminated the worry of overheating in the differential. (It's worth noting that in race work a Cobra differential will run gear ratios from 4.55 down to 3.07 depending on the type of track, race and driver.)

For driver protection a drive shaft guard, of reinforced ½" steel rod, is bent and welded to the two frame tubes at the rear of the transmission and over the drive shaft. Due to construction of the Cobra, and location of the drive shaft tunnel, the forward end of the drive shaft spins quite close to the driver's elbow. Should the shaft break the drive shaft guard would keep it from coming up through the floor of the car.

Another safety feature in racing Cobras was installation of a scatter shield and a nearly unbreakable bell housing to collect and contain flying fragments should the clutch or flywheel come apart in competition. Shelby American mechanics have tested the cast-steel bell by deliberately exploding flywheels and haven't broken one yet. The standard aluminum bell housing used on the street Cobra weighs about 14 lbs. less but with the tremendous power available in the Fairlane V-8, drivers consider their bodies far more valuable than eliminating a few pounds.

Racing type exhaust headers are constructed for Shelby American by Derrington in England. A single pipe coming out of each cylinder port collects into a four inch pipe and exhaust tube (one for each bank) underneath the car. They exit in front of the rear wheels with a 90° cutoff. The entire system is hung from the chassis on special brackets welded to the frame. The muffler and exhaust pipe system is rubber bushed to frame brackets with rubber so flexible that the exhaust system will shake and move as the body twists and the engine torques. Without this flexibility, bolts and mountings would be sheared off halfway through a race.

Construction of racing mufflers, required by some associations, is a simple matter. A 40″ cylinder of 5-inch tubing is placed around 40″ length of perforated 4-inch tubing, both of 1/16-inch wall stock. Flanges are made and the two welded together to create a simple cylinder within a cylinder. It creates no back pressure, as theoretically it is a straight pipe of 4-inch tubing passing through the 5-inch outer shell. The ½″ perforations in the center 4-inch tubing break up pulsations and provide a minimum muffling effect. There are two mufflers —one for each engine bank. Thus each cylinder exits into a 4-inch tube which passes from engine to tail pipe exit without hindrance or back pressure.

An important chassis modification is the mounting of bumper plates on the sides of the trunk well and on fender wells inside the engine compartment. They support race-type bumper pads and absorb vibration and jarring which could shake out regular bumper mounting bolts. Jack pads for a racing type jack, are a part of the bumpers. This pivot-type jack allows one man to quickly raise an end of the car with one swing of the handle.

A more unusual body modification is addition of valances on all fenders. FIA rules require that the axle hub of each wheel be inside a line dropped from the fender edge. Racing Cobras' oversize magnesium wheels and larger tires extended beyond production-model fenders and made the valances necessary to meet FIA regulations.

When the Cobras run at Sebring, number and recognition lights are required on the right side of the car so it can be identified as it passes the scorers. A license plate light is mounted on the door just above the number. Recognition lights are installed on the side and sometimes between headlights. These are coded colored lights, so that each pit crew can identify the car coming in. For night racing, heavy duty driving lights, which throw a tremendous beam, are mounted on the front of the car. They switch separately from the headlights and are wired into a separate circuit, so if anything happens to one light system the other would continue to function.

The most unusual modification is shortening of the front main spring leaf by $\frac{1}{2}$ to $\frac{5}{8}$ of an inch. The shortening is accomplished by rerolling the eyes at each end of the front transverse leaf which is mounted across the frame on an upright in the middle of the central forward cross member. In early racing Cobras the spring hanger would occasionally "work," allowing the spring to shift slightly and twist. This threw handling of the car completely off, to the point where drivers were aware that the front suspension assembly was shifting. Now, one of the modifications is to weld up "key" stock and make a channel in the spring hanger for the main leaf to drop into. Additional key stock is placed alongside the spring and wired to the A-frame. When the four U-bolts are tightened solidly the two plates that form the upper part of the U-bolt arrangement hold the entire assembly down on the A-frame.

After the engine has been installed in the car, all four wheels are aligned. Front wheels are set for $\frac{1}{8}''$ toe-in by adjusting the front steering rods. Rear wheels, independently suspended, are also set for $\frac{1}{8}''$ toe-in. This can only be done by bending rear cross members to change the position of the rear spring in order to get the proper toe-in. Caster and camber of front suspension is built into the car and cannot be changed without bending the frame or suspension members. There was a slight modification in camber, when the front spring was shortened, resulting in a slightly more negative camber to the front end.

Racing shock absorbers installed on the Cobras are made in Holland and pre-set mid-way in their range. Once at the track, it is up to the driver to decide how he wants the shock absorbers set. Much of this depends on track conditions and a driver's idea of how his car could handle. Each man has his personal preference. One likes a soft ride and feels the car handles better with softly sprung rear suspension and stiff in the front. Another driver might want it completely opposite with stiff shock absorbers in the rear and very soft on the front. On a track where there is a particular corner in which a wheel lifts and the rest of the run is fairly simple a driver may ask to have one wheel stiffened slightly, but this is unusual.

Sway bars in various diameters to create different tensions can be installed. The usual installation on a Cobra has the standard ¾" bar on front and the standard ⅝" bar in the rear. These dimensions are changed to meet driver preference, and some drivers, such as Ken Miles, prefer not to have sway bars at all. Dan Gurney likes both front and rear bars to be of ⅜" diameter to give only the very slightest sway control. The bars are not adjustable once installed, though their rubber sockets provide a certain amount of give before torsion effect of the bar begins to control body sway.

One man who has been literally up to his elbows in the race car program is Al Dowd, Service and Warranty Manager of the Shelby American Cobra project. Al has built Cobra race cars from completely stripped bare frames. We asked Al to tell us something about preparing cars for racing.

"One thing you have to keep in mind is that when you work on a race car you work twenty-four hours a day. Before Sebring, in 1963, there were ten of us here to work on four cars. Unfortunately we didn't get our new race chassis until about three weeks before we left. We'd split up with two or three of us on each car at a time. From nine in the morning—and we didn't get home until three or four the next. We'd get a couple hours sleep and come back and work some more —for the full three weeks before Sebring.

"When we thought the cars were ready we loaded them on our haulaway trucks. We had two of the older cars and two new ones, both of which used basically the same engine we are running in 1964. We sent the trucks off for Sebring; put all bits, pieces and parts in boxes; shipped them off, and flew down. The cars arrived about nine o'clock Tuesday night and we were to race Saturday. We started working the moment the cars were unloaded, and at eleven o'clock Thursday morning knocked off for the first time."

While they were working race circuits they occasionally found time to give other Cobra enthusiasts assistance. As Al explained it, "If we had our work done, and our cars in shape, we'd always give them the help they needed. Most of the boys have their own crews but every once in a while we have to give them a hand. When in trouble they all write us. We give them the information we have—developing new ideas to increase their chances of winning over the most severe competition."

One of the most unusual requests was from an owner who wanted Al to fly 2,000 miles and teach his pit crew to handle the new car in a race. This was an expense-paid trip, so Al went. When he arrived, he discovered there were no tools, no parts and the pit crew was a 12-year-old brother of the car owner! Luckily, the new car caused no trouble. With borrowed tools and a borrowed shop, Al was able to set it up so well the new car owner won his event.

We asked Al what a Cobra owner should do to a street vehicle in order to enter it in competition. "It depends upon the type of competition they want to enter," he said. "If they want to run the Cobra in a rally, a very little work will make it highly competitive. If they plan real road racing, I'd suggest they purchase one of our racing models.

"It's far cheaper for one thing. If they try to duplicate all the modifications you discuss in your book, they'll still have an inferior automobile and the price would be far above what they would pay for one of our race cars. However, I'd like to repeat that for a rally the car needs very little work; just tightening it up, changing some bolts to take care of the greater stresses, adding the oversize oil pan for a little extra oil, installing the oil cooler and using necessary lubricants for high speed and high stresses."

Al told us that the best thing to make a standard Cobra go better is to install the Cobra dual-manifold four-barrel carburetor setup plus a modified exhaust system to improve breathing. These are economical modifications which the owner can do himself. They give a street model Cobra all the beans anyone can use outside of all-out road racing competition.

Though each Cobra is delivered with many miles on the speedometer, put on by test drivers checking to insure perfection of performance, it is suggested that sustained speeds over 65 miles an hour not be undertaken during the first 500 miles driving. One of the reasons for this is that the car is delivered with break-in oil in the crankcase. After 500 mile margin, the Shelby American people recommend a good S.A.E. 10-30 weight for just about everything except frigid weather or extremely high temperatures such as desert heat over 100°.

Thirty pounds tire pressure all around is suggested as a good place to start. Some drivers prefer a soft ride and others a hard ride. In an area where there is quite a bit of mountain climbing, and curving roads, it is suggested that tire pressures be carried slightly higher to the 34 and 35 pound mark. For fast climbing, a higher pressure, say 38 pounds, is desirable. As most competition drivers know, if tire pressures are carried too low, it is possible to rip the tire off the rim in hard climbing turns. Thirty-eight pounds is considered about maximum for Cobra tires. Beyond that you won't have the full width of tread on the road.

An unusual maintenance feature about the Cobra is the need to occasionally remove wheels and change their position. This is known as "indexing" the hub. Wheels should be rotated periodically so they don't wear in one position on the hub splines. Another need is an occasional check of the spokes to keep them tight and true. This is not something a Cobra owner should undertake, as it requires an expert in wire wheel handling to modify the spokes. The easy way to check is to spin the wheel off the ground and touch the spokes with a screwdriver blade. Each should ring with about the same tone. If one sounds dull or high-pitched, it needs adjustment. Cobra wire wheels can be balanced either on the car or off. Disc brakes and hub assemblies are balanced at the factory and no additional indexing or balancing is required once wheels are set.

6. Engine Modification to Win

Ford V-8 engines are prepared for competition running in Carroll Shelby's Cobra, by Cecil Bowman, one of the nation's foremost production-engine tuners. For "Book of the Cobra", Cecil told Bill Carroll exactly what has been done to improve performance of Ford V-8 engines. Details were given on how he goes about modifying an engine for maximum performance and what he considers the most valuable techniques for maintaining a high performance engine in raceworthy condition.

* * *

Cecil, how many men do you have working in your shop?

We have four men in the engine shop now. One of our men is a specialist in disassembly and assembly of complete engines and capable of doing machine work for some of our special rebuilding jobs. Another specializes in porting, polishing and modification or fitting of valves and valve systems. A third man is an assembler. His sole job is assembly of V-8 engines prior to test and eventual racing. I run the dynomometer and do whatever assembly work is necessary to maintain a reasonable flow of raceworthy engines.

Did you do any work on the 260-cubic-inch version of the Fairlane V-8?

We only did a little on a dual carburetor installation. We changed manifolds and headers, camshafts, valve installation, the distributor curves, piston shapes and so forth to see what we could come up with as far as horsepower was concerned.

What kind of carburetors were you using?

We tried the four-barrel Holly carburetor and regular Ford carburetors. We even tried three two-barrels as well as two four-barrel Carters. We tried a blower, on the dyno, to see what we could come up with. It was an experimental unit that didn't work out to our satisfaction so we didn't go ahead with it.

What engine were the Ford carburetors from?

They were four-barrel carburetors from the 289-cubic-inch job. We put them on the 260 to see what would happen. The Holly carburetors were from the 260. We also tried two four-barrel Holly carburetors on a ram-tube manifold. It worked real good but was kind of complicated.

How would you describe headers you worked with on the 260-cubic-inch V-8?

On the 260 we had headers made by Ford. They were designed with two ports collecting into one pipe. That pipe, in turn, went into a common collector where the other pipe joined. It's a pretty good exhaust system, but compared to Cobra racing headers, it's no where near as effective. There's as much difference between the 260-cubic-inch header and our Cobra racing header as there is between the 260 header and a stock exhaust system.

When did you go to work on the 289-cubic-inch engines, Cecil?

I started work on the eighth or ninth 289 which was in progress when I arrived. By that time, they'd perfected and opened up the engine to give the proper bearing clearances. We came up with a few modifications for the oil pump, changed the head, valves, valve areas and upped the compression ratio a little. We've done a little experimentation with different camshafts in this one.

Do you do any checking on the engine before you install a different shaft?

We sure do. By the time a new shaft goes into an engine, I've checked it out and degree'd it to know what I want to start with. I'll always retain these figures. For example, if an engine has been put together so that it's four degrees off, we'll run it that way knowing that it's four degrees off on every setting we make. This is a part of the permanent engine record.

Cecil, is there any way you can check out an engine without putting a degree wheel on it?

I can check it while setting the valve lash. But the engine has to be all together. What you have to do is take a pair of dividers and run degree markings around the damper before you bolt it onto the crankshaft. You make a degree wheel out of the flywheel or front damper, starting with factory marks that are on there. But first we check the timing mark on the dampener itself, and run off the increments that are on there, to check them. You don't have to do very much of this. With 30 or 40 degrees on either side of top dead center, you have a pretty good degree wheel as far as checking valve timing is concerned.

You set your number one piston on top dead center to check it out?

That's right. Read it and find out where it's peaking and where your valves are. You can see that on the degree wheel. You actually have to go on the basis of watching valve action to see when it begins to start to open, and the point where you know it's closed. What you're doing is turning the engine over, watching the degree wheel and watching the valve action The moment the valve starts to open is when you'd be checking the degree markings on your flywheel or crankshaft.

Then you compare this with specifications for the engine?

Specifications for the engine and for the camshaft. You see, it's the cam you're interested in and what you want to check is the degree at which the cam begins to open. When factory engineers design an engine, and release specifications on it, they have what they believe is the best actual timing of the valve in relationship to efficiency of a specific engine. All you're doing is making sure that manufacturing errors have not crept into the assembly or marking, which would reduce efficiency of the power plant.

How do you check the cam timing?

I have a degree wheel that I use or I can check it with guages. By measuring action at the valve as to when it opens, and when it closes, in relationship to top dead center, we can use a degree wheel or crankshaft dampner markings to determine whether the engine is at its point of design efficiency. The degree wheel on a crankshaft tells you the position of the crankshaft and at which point the valve lift is supposed to be "x" thousandths of an inch. In this way, you can check out valve action in relation to optimum efficiency of the engine based on the designer's data.

You mentioned the importance of getting proper clearance. Where do you modify clearances?

We modify clearances on the crankshaft, that is, on main bearings and connecting rod bearings. We even like to get a little bit more clearance than ordinary between pistons and cylinder bores. As far as valve lash goes, we're very precise—and for all the bearings. We open them up a bit.

You said you modified the oil pump?

We give it a little bit more pressure by tightening down on the relief spring. Some time ago we had a breakage on the pump mounting which as you know attaches to the outside of the engine. Now we reinforce the outside to get away from vibration which occurs during competition. Then we put a baffle in the oil pump screen to reinforce it so that it will stand pressures that we generate at high engine rpms.

What about various types of piston pin fitting methods?

As you know, our regular piston pin is pressed into the rod. Your whole clearance around the pin is in the piston boss itself. We've tried what we call a "floating pin." We've reamed the rod out and put a bushing in it with clearance so the rod floats on the pistol pin. You can do this with certain pistons by putting end locks in the piston boss so that the pin is actually floating completely free. If you have a full skirted piston that's not a bad deal. With a regular Ford piston, or the type we use in our racing engine, to cut a lock groove into the boss is tough because it has to have plenty of meat for the end locks. If you're going to turn at real high speed, at a certain rpm, it's not too bad.

But under our conditions, it's not really necessary. The

way that the piston comes from Ford, in the high performance engine, is as good as any to go racing with. We've had no trouble with it. The only reason we've experimented has been to see what we could do in turning higher rpm. So far, it hasn't made much difference to use anything except what Ford provides.

What does an end-lock type piston do—reduce friction?

That's right. In a full floating piston, all wear is occuring where the pin floats in the end of the rod and in the piston bosses. Therefore, in an ordinary production car you can set your pins tighter in the piston. This is a pretty good idea because you'll have an engine that gives a lot longer mileage before becoming noisy. In racing, that's not absolutely necessary because you examine the pins after every race anyhow. Ordinarily we tear one down to look at it before we go into another race. We give extra clearance anyhow, so a little noise doesn't mean too much to us.

What kind of pistons did you experiment with?

I've had some Jahns "pop ups" and I've tried some Forged-True with a pop-top to give different compression ratios. Of course we've tried various sizes of the regular Ford aluminum pistons.

What's a "pop-up" piston?

A pop-up is a piston with a hump on the top that enters the combustion chamber to cut down its volume and increase compression ratio. This is its only purpose.

You mentioned a full-skirted and a slipper-type piston. How do these differ?

Usually a full-skirted piston has a full round skirt and is cam ground. A slipper piston usually has just the thrust side of the piston extending below the connecting rod boss. This portion of the skirt is all that's hitting the cylinder wall. Probably there's not more than a quarter of the piston touching the wall at any one time.

Would this reduce friction?

By far. You can have a closer fitting slipper piston than you can a full-skirted piston. Expansion in a piston, when heat hits it, is primarily at the full skirts. You have to allow for this cam-ground clearance to offset the expansion. With a slipper piston you don't have to allow so much clearance because some of the expansion wil be taken up into the head of the piston which is not touching the cylinder wall.

In changing cylinder heads and modifying them, what do you actually do?

We put bigger valves into our racing engines. We go to an 1-7/8" intake valve and a 1-5/8" exhaust valve. We mill out the heads so that they'll take these bigger valves which is to get better breathing. Then we port and polish all the galleys to accept the valves and the air-fuel mixture they'll pass. We work around the valve guides so that we can get the full amount of air that we can into the engine. The same port and polish methods are used so that we can get gas out through the exhaust system. We mill the head a little bit to get the compression ratio up. In addition, we work with valve area and combustion chambers size to equalize each cylinder so that they all have identical displacement. The only cutting we do on valve guides is through porting and modifying them for maximum air flow.

In working with the combustion chamber, how do you know where to begin?

We've been working with a flow bench here in the shop trying to change combustion chamber shapes without going into a new casting. What we're trying to do is change the way the engine will breathe or the amount of air that will go into a combustion chamber. Through our flow bench, we can tell how much air is going in. Sometimes we can change it just a little bit and get better breathing. As you know, it has to breathe to run.

What is a flow bench and how do you use it?

A flow bench it little more than a big suction pump. You attach your cylinder head to it, turn on the suction pump and measure the amount of air going through the head on a manometer. By reading the amount of air that goes in at various areas of valve opening, you can tell how efficient your engine is. The better the combustion chamber and the better the areas that you have developed, the more air you can get in the engine. It's just a matter of experimentation as far as the flow bench is concerned, because the better the engine breathes, the better it will run. As far as I'm concerned, every good engine shop should have a flow bench to find out what it is they're doing that's improving performance of the engine.

Do you put a complete engine on the flow bench or just cylinder head?

We usually run the head alone. We have a cylinder which duplicates the cylinder of a production engine. We fasten the head to the cylinder block with "O" rings. To evaluate valve action and efficiency, we open the valve by inserting shims between it and the rocker arm. In this way we duplicate cam action through the actual and complete opening cycle. All this time the flow bench is running and telling us on the manometer how much air is actually going through the combustion chamber. In a way, it's a duplication of a one-cylinder engine running.

We can actually measure air flow in the head all the way from the intake in the carburetor down to the exhaust system. It depends upon where we want to do our work. What's important is that even the shape of the valve will modify the readings. It could be a tulip valve or a flat type works best. Readings will tell us if we should run 45° seats or 30°, or what we should run. Every change will tell a story. They all vary over opening range of the valve. This way we can tell how much cam lift we should have. We can tell how much we have, what degree we want and other modifications that could lead to improved performance from the engine we're working on.

Generally speaking, when you use the flow bench, does air come in through the spark plug hole, or through the exhaust or intake valve?

It would come through the intake port and through the valve chamber just exactly as in an operating engine. If the spark plug holes are there, we put a plug in them. We can put a little spinner on the end of a special plug that tells us the amount of swirl in the air-fuel mixture entering the cylinder.

We even put a little color into the incoming air—spray color into it—to see where the air is going; or where it's hitting inside the combustion chamber before it's sucked out through exhaust ports by the fan on the flow bench.

How do you go about balancing combustion chambers so each one is identical?

That's done by milling. We also make minor changes by sinking or raising the valve. We change the relationship of the valve seat to the valve well, so that we can even up combustion chamber capacity. You've got to have it even if you're going to have an even running engine. If you don't have the same combustion chamber area in each one, you're going to have uneven power output. The amount the head is up into the cumbustion chamber reduces chamber volume. We don't modify valves very much unless they're way off in the first place. We can change combustion chamber capacity one or two ccs by raising or lowering the valve into the cylinder head.

Do you cut the valve head before you cut the seat?

We work it either way. Lots of times we take off a little at each place. Sometimes by taking just a little bit off of the valve seat, we can lower the valve and that won't affect the weight of the valves at all. It is really important that all valves be the same weight.

Do you use the Ford cam in your race cars?

We use the standard Ford camshaft (from the high performance 289 V-8 engine) in our racing cars. Ford makes a different cam for the standard 289, but this is their high-performance-engine camshaft.

You mentioned that you worked with valve springs. What did you do in that department?

We're still experimenting with valve springs. What we're trying to do is get the proper seat pressure, and proper open pressure, for some of the experimental cams we've been playing with. All of these have different lifts and we've tried to come up with a spring that's soft enough so that the camshaft isn't worn. There's a lot of difference in spring balance and a difference in the spring that we use as related to the rpm we run our engines.

What's the story on spring bounce?

Most people call it valve float but it's really a harmonic in the springs. When a valve spring hits a harmonic the spring starts "dancing." It's not seated and will dance up and down and finally, in a certain range of engine revs, the spring coils are hitting each other. When that happens you don't get a true rhythm in opening and shutting of the valve.

Are you using single or double springs in your experimental work?

We have used them both. If we can come up with a single spring with a damper in it, it would be the best possible spring for our use. The trouble with double springs is that usually the center spring is used for dampning but it gives you friction and heat. You have a lot of pressures that are unnecessary a lot of the time with double springs, but a lot of fellows have to use them just to get by with the camshafts they're running. You see, in racing, you don't need as much spring pressure as you do in dragging where you don't run for any great length of time. If you run an engine over a 500-mile race with dual springs in the valve train, heat and friction eventually break down the valve springs. Near the end of the race, spring tension is not nearly as effective as it was at the start.

You're speaking of heat build-up as a result of the spring?

Of the spring's flexing. The inner spring rubbing against the outer spring is where the trouble begins. You see, we have to fit them so close there's almost an interference fit between the coils. The main reason for fitting the inner spring is so it will act as a damper which is trying to stop the harmonics. That's the only purpose we have for that one. As far as I'm concerned, for our type of racing, a single spring on the valve would be the best thing we could use.

Do you do any work inside the mainfolds in cleaning or port matching?

On everything we run, we've always got to match them.

We put gaskets on every one of them and match so we know we're not blocking the flow of gasses.

How would I make a "gasket match?"

In the first place, put your intake manifold gasket on a port of the head and then draw around on the inside where it is going to be. Do the same thing on the intake manifold. Use a stone or a grinder of some sort to cut out the port so they match and you'll get a full and free flow of gas. Just use the gasket as a template, then scribe your lines.

You said you worked with headers. Can you tell me a little bit about what you did with them on the 289 V-8?

We tried the collector type where each exhaust port has a separate tube that runs out and collects into a common collector pipe. All four of them run into this collector pipe and then the exhaust pipe takes off from the end of the collector Y.

The 289 is a real good header. In fact, they're practically the same thing as our racing headers except they're all in cast iron. The proper lengths are cast into a common collector and run into a funnel of the manifold itself. They're similar to the big racing headers that stock cars run at Daytona only they're a little smaller to fit our 289 engines.

What is the Cobra racing header like?

We call the Cobra racing header "spaghetti." It's a tube-like affair with crossovers that we need because of the firing order of the engine. We designed it so that one exhaust pulse is not bucking another and will go separately through the exhaust pipes or funnels. That's where the difference is from other types of headers. In the working range of the engine it gives a lot better horsepower. We've not been able to run it on the dyno yet but on ordinary track circumstances, in the working range of from 5000-7000 rpms, we estimate gaining anywhere from 15 to 20 extra horsepower.

You mentioned working with the intake manifolds. What type of work did you do with these?

The present intake manifold we have on the regular race cars is as good as any other as far as we're concerned. We've experimented though with aluminum four barrels and we've had four-throat manifolds with the ram tube system. We tried some dual Carters on the 289 but didn't got a sufficient degree of improvement to justify the trouble. Our Weber carburetors are strictly for the racing cars. We made the manifold itself and that's what we've been using to get the best performance out of the engine.

When Weber carburetors are installed on the competition engine it is necessary to make a special type of linkage arrangement to operate them. A bracket is bolted onto the rear of the left cylinder head using Hilborn throttle arms with aircraft-type friction-free bearings. We fabricate a linkage setup that allows operation of the carburetors without linkage loss. It is only built for the Weber carburetors of the full house race machine. The roller bearings of the Hilborn system eliminate any friction and maintain a solid linkage connection between the driver's throttle foot and the throttle blades. With this installation about an inch and a half of travel of the accelerator pedal will open the throttle blades a full 90 degrees.

Aside from the Weber Carburetor setup, what changes do you make in carburetors to get maximum performance from standard Ford engines?

I usually go into them to make sure jetting is right and they're up to specifications. Then I see that the float level is right. I make no changes or adjustments for the secondaries; I just want to make sure of when they're going to come in. There's no problem here as this Ford 4-barrel carburetor is made and calibrated for this high performance engine.

What do you do with the fuel pumps?

There's a real good fuel pump on the Ford V-8 and it'll carry the fuel. In fact, it carries as much fuel as we need for the eight Webers that we tried. You've got all the gas you need on this engine.

Do you do anything with the water pump?

On the Cooper Cobras, we cut down the fins because we're running at such high engine speed. We taken every other fin off to reduce cavitation. We don't change anything else. It just runs real good for high speed racing of this machine.

What about the use of pressurized radiator caps?

They're mighty important. In racing you have to have a pressurized radiator system. We pressurized ours to find out how strong it was. In racing, going down on a fast stretch, you might be getting high heat with high head temperatures. When you're slowing down, you come down and cool real fast. With expansion and contraction and the water changing its level you've got to have a pressurized cap or you'll lose all your water pretty doggone quick. On racing machines, we don't use a fan.

Do you have any opinion on the slip fans with viscous drive?.

They seem to be real good and actually they save a lot of horsepower at high speed. There's a lot of people just taking the fan off and putting a couple of blowers on to keep the radiator cool when it's idling.

Do you like fan belts tight or loose?

I like mine tight. I don't want to throw one so I usually put pretty good tension no it. In the King Cobra and the Cooper, we have changed the position of the pump, by making different clearances on the end of the frame, so we run the belt pretty tight. I always like to make sure they're in line. We check that very closely so they're not running out of line.

How much difference do you figure the alternator makes to drag on the engine?

There's a lot of argument about that but there's a lot of drag in a generator. I consider it enough to make a real difference though we haven't run any test on this yet.

Do you make any changes in size of the pulleys or depth of their groove?

No, we haven't on the standard Cooper or the racing Cobras. But on the Cooper Cobra, we've modified both the water pump and alternator pulley. We made them a bit larger so the pump and alternator turn a bit slower.

Do you do any work with ignition systems?

Oh, yes, we've done quite a bit of work on the ignition system. With the old distributor a pin holding the drive gear at the bottom of the shaft would shear off. Then we found that the advance curve wasn't just exactly right to get maximum performance out of the V-8 engine. We've come up with a real good advance curve that does the job. Then too we're using a dual-point distributor with extra tension on the points. With dual points you get good dwell and heat doesn't take spring life away from the breaker point arms. There's more life and points are lasting a lot longer.

Do you make any changes in the ignition wiring?

We use regular Autolite ignition wiring as far as the spark plug wires are concerned because it's more heat resistant than anything else we can find. It has a stainless steel wire core. The set on the Ford high-performance engine is good wire but the ends are not quite as securely attached as those from Autolite. I'm speaking now about the ends over the hood of the spark plug. Heat will often affect those and dry them out so you have to replace them.

What about spark plug type or choice?

We've experimented some with those. The spark plug choice has to be by heat range as related to what we're running in carburetion. After all, a spark plug has to be cool to be effective. As of now, we're using Autolite spark plugs of the extended-tip type. It's similar to the original plug that comes with the car but it's an outside heat range.

You mentioned that you're very precise on valve clearance. Why is this?

Valve clearances have everything to do with valve timing and valve timing changes the torque curve of an engine. You either retard or advance the whole valve mechanism by the way the valve is opening or closing.

Let's assume you have too much valve lash. What have you done to the engine?

What you've actually done is retarded your camshaft. It won't give you less torque. It merely changes torque from a low rpm to a higher rpm. Closing up your valve lash will actually bring your torque curve down to a lower rpm range.

What do mechanics mean by "running" the valves?

What I mean by running is to adjust them cold: cold because

Dave McDonald hangs his Cobra way out during a hot lap at the Dodger Stadium races held in March of 1963. McDonald won the event, followed by Ken Miles in another Cobra.

valve lash changes as heat build up. So I set cold, then I run the engine plenty hard so I know, after it's hot, the valve set has hardened and will stay where it's supposed to be. After it's taken it's set, and reached its maximum heat through a run, I adjust valves to the point where I want this particular engine for maximum performance. This will be marked down so we know that, for this particular engine, it must always be set in this fashion for maximum power output.

Do you run the valves again?

I run through them again with feeler gauges and then set them. I do that because heat will change the lash. It could either open them or it could close them. I set them after it is on the dynamometer and the engine is at running temperature as a slow rpm. You have to run it to keep the temperature up. If the engine is in a chassis, you may run it on the road and come back and let it idle while you go through the valves. Then you can tell, before your heat actually changes, what the valve lash is and what is should be.

Let's go over this method of setting valve lash again, to make sure I understand it properly.

Well, I always set the valves cold according to designer's specifications until the engine is run. But before I do this, I check the cam timing. This gives me a better idea of what valve lash I want. I find that in most production cams, no matter who grinds them, the overlap is about the same. But all cam timing is not. Evidently, they don't put the cam billet in the lathe in the right place so that you don't always get the same valve timing on every cam although it is supposed to be the same. So I always check the cam first and degree it to find out where I want to set the valves. You see, we can vary production timing as much as .0010 of an inch by making changes in the valve lash.

If you thought valve timing could be improved, what would you do to valve lash to get maximum torque at low speeds?

I would open the valves maybe about .002 further. Then I'd check it out to see if that's where I really wanted it. If it was in a car, I'd drive it. Low speed torque would be real good in traffic and a lot better for economy. Once you've reached the minimum speed you're going to run, then you're actually into the performance curve of the engine. Your engine is just lazy-ing along but you've got to get up there. The quicker you get to this point, the better off you are. Then you can ease back on your throttle and it's better for your car. The wider you can set a valve, the better economy you're going to get, if you're not going to run the engine at excessive speeds.

Now if you have the same engine and you want high-speed torque to increase your performance, would you tighten up the valve lash?

I would tighten it up, but not to the point of burning the valves. There's a given maximum for every camshaft. Every cam is made to operate with a certain amount of clearance. Some cams can do with a little less and some can't. You can close down a little bit on most cams and the ramps will be okay to keep it running. I would only change it .002 at a time to keep track of modifications and not become erratic in my tuning.

If someone you knew owned a Ford V-8 260 or 289, and wanted to make it really go, what would you tell him to do?

In the first place, I'd find out what he's going to use it for. If he's going to run it in competition, I'm afraid I wouldn't tell him too much. We get a lot of calls from fellows who want to run them for drag strips and I just try to help them out with bearing clearance information and advice. I tell them how to calibrate and modify distributor curves for the best power output for maximum acceleration.

The first thing they ask me is about carburetion. I tell them to run it as is. Usually they want to get a different spring on the secondary throttle blades. They think they have to hear them open but that's not true. All you have to do is disconnect the secondary and find out it isn't true. It is opening whether they can hear it or not.

What would you suggest he do to his ignition?

He's going to have to use the regular high-performance ignition system with the Ford 289 and set it up into the curve where his engine is capable of running its best. It's important he not worry about the initial start of the distributor but get where maximum power is—at the point he's going to run his engine. Full advance of the distributor should take place about the same time that the scondaries open on the carburetor.

What other engine changes would you suggest?

There's not much you can do for the 289 except go to a full race engine. From the 260-cubic-inch V-8 you can pick up a tremendous amount of horsepower. Just make sure you have a good valve job, that your ports are matched and clearances are proper. You can pick up a lot of horses on that. The main thing from my point of view is—don't alter anything on a 289.

What about the exhaust? Would you suggest he change the mufflers?

The exhaust systems—that is the headers they have on the 289—are exceptionally good. I wouldn't advise changing the mufflers because there's not that much difference in them.

What about the use of air scoops or vents to increase ventilation of the engine?

There again you run into the question of what you're going to use the car for. If you have a lot of high-speed running, or go into racing, then you have to get the air out of there to keep the engine cool. If you draw the heat off, the engine will be cool but you've got to create a low pressure area someplace to get that hot air out from under the hood.

Vents in the back of the engine compartment, rather than in front of the engine, will do the job. The engine compartment is what I'm talking about now, not the radiator.

What about the hood scoops?

Hood scoops are all right, but they're merely getting air in. You can hurt yourself sometimes because you create a pressure undernearth your hood unless you've got plenty of openings to get the hot air out. Louvered hoods are fine for beauty, but you have to have a place for air to get out. Usually there's not enough opening in the bottom or around the engine at the back end. If you create pressure underneath the hood, and if it's not blowing the right way, you're going to lose carburetion efficiency.

What sort of maintenance would you pay most attention to for a high-performance 289 or 260?

Obviously you have to keep it tuned. As far as bearings or mechanical parts are concerned, if you've kept it oiled and haven't overheated or over-revved, this Ford V-8 is a long-lasting engine with a good life. We have a real good history on our racing engines. As far as I'm concerned, all you have to worry about on maintenance is keeping it well tuned and seeing that oil is right, and valves are set properly. Plugs, timing, distributor, carburetion and valve lash of course, should be checked after every race.

Would you recommend that Ford owners wanting to improve efficiency of their engine experiment with their valve settings or leave them alone?

I'd say it would be a good idea—and don't go overboard—

to try a couple of degrees on one side and a couple of degrees on the other to see if it improves the performance. If an engine that should be set at .019 is set at .021 it only moves your torque curve. It won't make much difference in total horsepower under ordinary circumstances. Unless you're going to drive at a given speed for a given time and never run it much over or under, it couldn't make a bit of difference. Most drivers could never tell it. But if you have a set speed that you're going to run, say from L.A. to Chicago at 42 miles an hour, it may help. We do this on the Mobilgas economy run. When you know that you're going to run the engine only at maximum efficiency, a thousandth of an inch valve lash can make quite a difference. But where you're changing car speed from 30 to 60 and back to 30 in ordinary driving, you'll never notice the difference.

In the case of the 42 miles an hour what you're doing is setting the valve lash to move the torque curve of the engine to the 42-mile-an-hour rpm mark?

To where the engine is really at its peak of performance. I have been working on the Mobil economy run for seven years and believe me, valve lash is one of the important things we worry about.

What do you consider "going overboard" when setting valve lash on a production engine?

Oh, to go really way out like a real wide lash or a real closed up lash. I would start somewhere near the specifications that the manufacturer calls for. By going a few thousandths one way or the other you might get a little better performance out of it. You can figure that if the manufacturer calls for .019 which is probably the minimum you'd want, .017 or .021 isn't going to make too much noise or trouble unless you're going to run it at real high speeds. Actually, valve lash is strictly for performance, though you have to have it set reasonably loose for cooling. If you reduce valve lash completely then you couldn't cool your valves. They'd never hit the seat when they got hot.

Do you recommend using new spark plugs for every race?

Not necessarily. It depends on how far they've been run. Take a look at the spark plugs and see how "well" they are. If you're using a new set of plugs for practice and you haven't run into difficulty, keep on running them.

At most races today, a spark plug company representative is on hand. If you can't read plugs yourself, you can have him read them for you. He'll tell you whether you're running hot or cold or whether you have detonation. There's a dozen different things he can tell you about engine performance from spark plug tip appearance.

What can one do with tuning?

Make sure that spark advance and distributor curve are set properly in the first place and remain that way. You also have to make sure that you have the proper percent of dwell on your breaker points in addition to the right breaker clearance. The advance curve must be right to begin with.

What about breaker gaps, Cecil?

On the dual point ignition systems, we run a wide gap and keep dwell high so the points will cool. The breaker points will burn up if they get too close and get hot. We want a high saturation in the coil and we can get it with dual points. We couldn't get this high saturation in a single point system. There, if you want saturation, the points would be so close that over a long race, they'd heat up and go bad. When an ignition system has dual points, we can get a wide gap (for cooling) and still get coil saturation we want.

Width of the gap is important because again, that's the saturation of the coil—the amount of the spark that you're running into. The time the breaker points are closed and the amount they're open controls the saturation in the cell. As far as I'm concerned, that is as important in tuning as anything else.

Would you recommend working the breaker points toward the closed side or along the open side?

The higher the saturation, the better you are and the better spark you have. In other words, the closer you have the points the greater the saturation; but you can go too far. I wouldn't recommend going over three percent closed—that is three percent dwell closed—over what is recommended. Then you have to check it every so often because your rubbing block will wear. As it wears, it will gradually close the points. You should check them if you run close. Otherwise, you'll burn your points because they're closing up.

For carburetion, what do you have to do to keep an engine well-tuned?

Actually, keeping a carburetor tuned is little more than seeing there's not any dirt. Once you set the carburetor, outside of dirt or ordinary fill up, it will stay pretty well in tune. Of course, there are mild adjustments for idle speed and mixture to make up for changes in altitude or weather.

Would you give me some examples of different uses for different secondary throttle cut-in time settings?

A lot of drivers like to stand on it and have the secondaries come in quicker. Many of these Ford engines have been put into races where the drivers like to go out on a drag strip and run them in the stock class. When you do that, you want the secondaries to come in at a certain place. This Ford carburetor has air velocity controlling the opening of the throttle blades which is a lot better than manual or electric linkage. When your engine is breathing right, the carburetor takes care of itself. It's as good a four-barrel carburetor for this engine as we've ever found.

If secondaries are velocity controlled, what is the mechanical means of modification?

Velocity control is through a tube that passes through the venturi on the carburetor barrel which opens the secondary. The control is a spring that holds the secondary throttle valve shut. If you change resistance of the spring, you can bring the blades in early or late. You can't take too much off the spring or weaken it in any way because if you do, when you want the blades to shut off, they won't shut properly. In making adjustments you've got to watch yourself on that.

What can you do to the velocity tube to change the cut-in time?

Don't do anything to the tube. Leave it alone. It's built right with the carburetor. To change secondary cut-in time work only with the spring. A little bit at a time because if you cut too much off, then your throttle won't return. You might want to back off on the throttle and the engine wouldn't slow down and idle properly. It wouldn't cut off like it does on the regular carburetors.

For race tuning, is there much difference in fuels?

I know that in different parts of the country we have to tune for local fuel. I always take different jetting along with us which we try to match with the fuel. We read spark plugs and modify jetting so that we run what we consider is the proper mixture. Sometimes you miss and sometimes you hit, but different parts of the country have different fuels and there is considerable difference as far as we are concerned.

What about ducting cool air to the carburetor intake?

We usually run with air horns on the racing Webers which extend up to the hood. On regular Cobras we have air scoops in front—two of them—that pull colder air to the carburetors. On the Coopers the air horns are up into the air stream so that we're getting plenty of fresh air. It's really important that we get cool air.

What about control linkages? Is it better that they be run oiled or dry?

Linkages should always be free. You have to check them at all times to see that they are properly oiled. I always put a drop of oil on all the joints so that they are free. If you get a sticky one, and then set up the carburetor, it's not right. You go out on the road and come back and they've changed. If it's free when you start, then you know what you've got every time. You can get a closer setting on your engine doing the tune up with completely free linkage.

What is your thinking on the type of engine oil to use?

I can't tell you what kind of oil to use. All major oil companies have a really good oil. They've had it checked and run by the factory so it's all right for the engine. You can usually tell by what's on the can that it will meet the manufacturer's specifications or will exceed them. If the manufacturer of the engine recommends the oil, it's good.

How do you read oil temperature in relation to the need for thicker or thinner oil in an engine?

That's where you really need to know how to read temperature. If you're using too thick an oil, it won't flow through the bearing fast enough. It stays in the bearing so long it heats up.

Your oil would be running hot and the pressure would be staying up. On the other hand, you might be running a thin oil through the bearings so fast that it would never have a chance to cool. There's not enough body in thin oil, so it's going to heat up. In this case, you have low oil pressure with high oil temperature. If you had a situation such as low oil pressure and high oil temperature or extremely high oil pressure and high oil temperature, you might be on the outside limits of where you want to go. You should be in the middle of these two extremes of lubrication.

What about choice of oil weight for different types of competition?

There have been a lot of arguments about that. Today, drivers have started changing ideas of weight. They used to think that we had to run an excessively heavy oil. The oil we use today has changed so much that we're not just exactly sure what they're running. In racing, we used to consider that it was an absolute necessity to run heavyweight oil, but today most drivers start and run on lighter oil—40 or 50 weight. A lot of fellows are running multiple viscosity oil. You wouldn't have heard of that five or ten years ago.

Let's move to carburetion, Cecil. What's the rule in tuning carburetors for high altitudes?

Actually you have to go for air-fuel ratio. By reading spark plugs, you'll find that you have "leaned out" considerably over what you had at sea level. You don't have the velocity of air coming in. The amount of air mixed with the fuel is so much less that you are leaning the carburetor. So, you have to go to a richer mixture. I usually run my carburetor float at the low level because in checking, you'll find that fuel pressure variations will change the float level. Suppose you set the float level on the full side at a specific spot. Then, if you're running high fuel pressure, it will build up just a little bit. So I usually check my float level on the low-side setting so that the build-up will be just about right.

In setting the air-fuel ratio, I try to go to a lean-max-power and then richen it. If you run lean-max-power, your engine runs hot. For my book, this isn't always the best place to run—it's on the ragged edge. If you do that, pretty soon you're going to blow a piston or something. Actually you richen the mixture to cool the engine.

Are there any changes to ignition in changed altitude?

If you can get the proper mixture to run well, you don't have to bother the ignition. By the same token, if you can't get the proper mixture, then you have to change ignition timing for that specific altitude. If you're fuel rich, you can ride higher degrees of advance than you can if you're running lean.

Would you change the heat range of your spark plugs?

I usually do. I carry about three different heat ranges. It would depend upon what I have to do to get the proper reading. It also depends if I can get the proper jet reading for the carburetor. You can change either one and get a different story altogether.

Do I read you right—that at a higher altitude, with a lean-hot fuel mixture, you might have to go to a colder plug?

Yes. Because you've actually leaned out. If you've leaned your carburetor to this thin air, then you have to go to a different plug. The engine is actually going to run hot. It's a hot mixture so you have to go to a colder plug to offset this. If you went to a place with high humidity, you might have to go to a warmer plug. This would be the more logical thing to do than to go to a colder heat range spark plug.

What is your opinion of transistorized ignition systems?

We haven't worked with them yet but I think that we'll

all come to it. The reason that transistorized ignitions are going to be so great is the same heat problem on breaker points I talked about before. With a transistorized system, you can have a real high coil saturation without overheating the points. Eventually, we'll never be concerned with maintenance of the distributor and it will be closed against tampering.

What is your opinion of additives in engine oils?

I'm not too strong on them. They've not been able to prove to me that—for racing—they've got it. They may be the greatest thing in the world, but I have to see it first.

Cecil, is there anything else you'd like to tell me about Cobra V-8 engines?

When they come from the factory, they're probably the finest production engines that I've ever seen. With a small amount of modification, they've already proved they're one of the most durable race engines we have in the world today. We're happy with them.

FAIRLANE V-8 ENGINE SPECIFICATIONS

	221 Two-Throat Standard	260 Two-Throat Standard	289 Two-Throat Standard	289 Four-Throat High Performance
Displacement, Cubic Inches Carburetion Standard or High Performance				
Type	90°-V8	90°-V8	90°-V8	90°-V8
Valve Arrangement	O.H.V.	O.H.V.	O.H.V.	O.H.V.
Bore	3.50"	3.80"	4.00"	4.00"
Stroke	2.87"	2.87"	2.87"	2.87"
Piston Displacement	221	260	289	289
Standard Compression Ratio	8.7-1	8.4-1	8.6-1	10.9-1
Maximum Compression Ratio		8.8-1	9.0-1	11.6-1
Max. bhp at rpm	145 @ 4400	164 @ 4400	195 @ 4400	271 @ 6000
Max. torque at rpm	216 @ 2200	258 @ 2200	282 @ 2400	314 @ 3400
Recommended Fuel	Regular	Regular	Regular	Premium
Idle Speed—Manual	400-525	575-600	575-600	700-800
Idle Speed—Automatic	400-500	475-500	475-500	N.A.
Piston Material	Aluminum	Aluminum	Aluminum	Aluminum
Piston Weight, oz.	17.28-17.42	18.76	21.27	21.09
Clearance, Top Land	.0120-.0158	.017-.0208	.035-.0427	.035-.0427
Piston Pins	SAE 5015-Steel	SAE 5015-Steel	SAE 5015-Steel	SAE 5015-Steel
Type	Press Fit	Press Fit	Press Fit	Press Fit
Clearance	.0001-.0003	.0003-.0005	.0003-.0005	.0003-.00045
Connecting Rods	Forged-SAE 1041	Forged-SAE 1041	Forged-SAE 1041	Forged-SAE 1041
Weight, oz.	18.50-18.89	19.97	19.97	20.77-21.05
Bearing Clearance	.004-.0018	.0011-.0027	.0009-.0029	.0019
Crankshaft Material	Molded Cast Iron	Molded Cast Iron	Molded Cast Iron	Molded Cast Iron
End play	.004-.008	.004-.008	.004-.008	.004-.008
Bearing clearance, main	.0006-.0020	.0009-.0028	.0007-.0030	.0006-.0027
Journal diameter	2.1232-2.1240	2.123	2.123	2.123
Camshaft material	Cast Iron	Molded Iron	Molded Iron	Molded Iron
Lifters	Hydraulic	Hydraulic	Hydraulic	Solid
Rocker ratio	1.60-1	1.60-1	1.60-1	1.60-1
Clearance, Intake				.020 (Hot)
Clearance, Exhaust				.020 (Hot)
Intake, Opens	21° BTDC	21° BTDC	20° BTDC	44° BTDC
Intake, Closes	51° ABC	51° ABC	66° ABC	82° ABC
Intake, Duration	252°	252°	266°	306°
Exhaust, Opens	57° BBC	57° BBC	56° BBC	92° BBC
Exhaust, Closes	15° ATC	15° ATC	20° ATC	34° ATC
Exhaust, Duration	252°	252°	256°	306°
Overlap	36°	36°	40°	78°
Intake Lift	.380	.380	.368	.4774
Exhaust Lift	N.A.	.380	.380	.4774
Outer Spring Pressure, open	170 Lbs.	161-177 Lbs.	161-177 Lbs.	247 Lbs.
Inner Spring Pressure, open	—	—	—	4-7 Lbs.

120

Oil Pump Type	Rotor	Rotor	Rotor	Rotor
Oil Pressure, Lbs. @ rpm	45-55 @ 2000	50-60 @ 2000	50-60 @ 2000	50-60 @ 2000
Capacity of crankcase, quarts	4	4	4	4
Exhaust pipe, Branch	1.62"	1.88"	1.88"	2.00"
Exhaust pipe, Main	1.75"	2.00"	2.00"	2.50"
Tail pipe	1.75"	2.00"	2.00"	2.25"
Fuel pump Pressure	4.5-5.5 p.s.i.	4.5-5.5 psi	4.5-5.5 psi	4.5-5.5 psi
Carburetor, Make	Ford	Ford	Ford	Ford
Barrels	Two	Two	Two	Four
Barrel size, Primary	1-5/16"	1-7/16"	1-9/16"	1-1/8"
Barrel size, Secondary	—	—	—	1-3/16"
Choke Type	Automatic	Automatic	Automatic	Automatic
Engine cranking Speed	180 rpm @ 80° F	180 rpm @ 80° F	180 rpm @ 80° F	180 rpm @ 80° F
Starter Torque (lbs. Ft.)	15.5	15.5	15.5	15.5
Breaker gap, Distributor	.014-.016	.014-.016	.014-.016	.019-.021
Cam angle, Distributor	26°-28.5°	26°-28.5°	26°-28.5°	30°-33°
Timing @ rpm, Ignition	6° @ 500	6° —	6° —	10° —
Spark Plug (Autolite)	BF-92	BF-42	BF-42	BF-32
Clutch Plate Pressure (Lb.)	1230	1278	1278	1585
Diameter, outside	9.5"	10.0"	10.4"	10.4"
Total Area (Sq. In.)	85.22	85.5	103.7	103.7

Comparison of specifications between the original 221-cubic-inch V8, the 260 and two 289s, discloses a series of power-providing modifications.

Bore has grown a half inch, from the 221 to 289, while stroke has remained the same. Compression ratios vary in modest increments, though power output has almost doubled in these production engines. Clearances of pistons and wrist pins have been increased to reduce internal friction of the larger engines. At the same time, connecting rods have become heavier to withstand power pulses of high performance versions of the Fairlane V8.

It's worth noting that the same molded cast iron crankshaft is used for all four engines, though main bearing clearances are slightly greater in the larger displacement block.

Greater evidence of modification is in the camshaft. Though the 221 and 260 used the same shaft, the mild 289 and the high performancce 289 have shafts with great overlap and duration.

Increases in carburetion show in barrel size comparison between the 221, 260 and basic 289. The high performance 289 uses a four-throat carburetor for maximum high speed output. Exhaust pipe changes closely relate to carburetor size to provide improved breathing relative to gas flow.

121

Ford Fairlane V8 engine, which has been used in the Cobra as a powerplant of 260 and 289 cubic inch displacement.

7. Ken Miles Discusses the Competition Cobra

One of the nation's most skilled competition drivers, Ken Miles, has racked up impressive victories driving the Cobras of Carrol Shelby. Here are his candid comments regarding this outstanding sports car.

Ken, now that you've handled the competition version of the Cobra, what is your opinion of it?

The race version of the Cobra is by any standards a hairy, fire-breathing monster. It offers a great deal more power than the street version, power it is capable of handling if the driver is reasonably discreet. Except for competition changes, the race and street versions are basically the same. The competition engine puts out more power and tires are bigger, but they have the same chassis, same transmission, same clutch, same rear end, and same axle shaft. The real difference is that the race engine is more highly tuned and in order to transmit this extra power to action it has to have more rubber on the ground.

But I won't kid you. The race machine is a handful in any language. The engine has an enormous amount of torque which makes it very easy to spin rear wheels at any time. In fact, you can spin both rear wheels as easily at a hundred miles an hour as when the car is sitting still. You've got to be reasonably careful about driving the thing. You could be going into a 120-mile-an hour corner, give the competition Cobra too much throttle and spin into trouble. You have to be really careful.

With the special wheels we use for racing, you have a great deal more offset between king-pin axis and tire center line. Accordingly, the steering wheel is extremely active. On a bumpy course you have your hands full. The brakes are absolutely superb under any circumstances. They're very, very good indeed and the transmission is one of the best. The four-speed all synchromesh ratios are fine. The only problem you have with a Cobra in competition is controlling the amount of power you've got. In fact, the same thing applies to a Cobra on the street. You've got to be reasonably discreet.

What do you feel is the best driving position for serious competition?

The ideal driving position is, unfortunately, in this day and age unobtainable. In my opinion it's a position where you're sitting reasonably upright with arms in a relatively relaxed position almost straight out so you can turn the steering wheel from full lock one way to full lock the other way without having elbows bang into your chest. It's important to sit up straight so you can see the contact point of both front wheels on the ground. I think this particular driving position went out about 1950. They haven't built cars like that for a good many years.

Nowadays in order to get the frontal area down, designers have to get the driver down inside the car, which means he can't see. In many cases drivers can't see the wheels at all, let alone the contact point. Cars are getting lower and more difficult to drive all the time, but there is nothing we can do about it because the designers are trying to reduce frontal area. Therefore, they put the driver lower and recline him more and more until he is practically lying on his back looking between his knees! It's inconvenient but inherent in design of the modern race car. You'll find in a car built to FIA specifications that even the minimum windshield is such that you can get a driving position which is fairly comfortable and with reasonable visibility. This is the way the Cobra is built. It is not so extreme as many of the more exotic racing cars.

How about the clutch pedal? Do you prefer it wide or narrow?

It's all a question of room. If the designer has room for it, "Yes." I like a wide pedal. You see, most cars are built *down* to FIA minimum specifications as far as cockpit room is concerned. By the time you put a great big gear box and clutch housing between your feet and the passenger's, you're more concerned about getting your feet in there at all than having extra room. It's a question of what you can do with the space available. If there's plenty of room, I like a great big pedal. It reduces unit loading area on the ball of the foot. In many cars, and the Cobra is one, you don't have that much room, so you're stuck with a rather narrow pedal and callouses on your feet.

In the Cobra competition model, what seating modifications would you suggest?

Anyone but a relatively short driver will find the standard seat that comes in the Cobra is far too high even to drive on the street. I prefer a lower seat, with a good deal less padding in it, than the one in the Cobra. The seat I use for competition has no padding whatsoever. It's just a fiberglas shell, low and reclining so that my shoulders are a long way under the rear roll of the body shell. This enables me to lie back in a relaxed position with my arms absolutely straight out. I can turn the steering wheel conveniently without having my elbows drop. The regular Cobra driver's seat is a lot more suitable for driving on the highway than for racing. In competition you have a different situation calling for a much lower seating position. Of course, there's no such thing as one ideal seat for every man.

Theoretically, for best vision in competition, the higher the seat the better. And the closer you can see to the front of the car the better. Practically, we find that if we design cars with the driver lower down, we can reduce the area of the windshield and therefore reduce wind resistance of the car and increase its speed. I shouldn't say it quite that way as we don't literally reduce the area of the windshield. What we do is lean it back further and give the car a better aerodynamic shape.

What about seat belts for competition driving?

It depends entirely upon the car you're in. If you're driving a Cobra in competition, you should have the regular Cobra roll bar installed. It's a great deal stronger than it looks, and very well fitted. With the roll bar the ideal arrangement would be to wear a lap belt and shoulder harness. You'll find that a shoulder harness installation, which hooks into the same clip release as the lap belt, is a very satisfactory arrangement. It will hold you down in the car so that you have excellent protection if the car rolls over.

The lap belt by itself is better than nothing at all, but doesn't provide adequate protection unless it is extremely tight. It serves another function in keeping the sides of the seat from bulging out, as well as keeping the driver rigidly held in one place. I believe that the more intimate the contact of my body with the car the better I can feel what's going on. I think seat belts are a great help under any circumstances.

A single exception might be in a very flimsy car like the Formula I racers. There a belt is probably more of a liability than an asset. In an accident in such an extremely lightweight super sports car, your only chance of surviving the crash is to be thrown clear. Formula cars are so lightly constructed they crumple like a crushed egg when they hit something and you don't want to be in them.

Ken, what type of crash helmet or conformation of helmet is best to wear in competition?

I don't think it's particularly critical as to the type helmet you wear. I believe the crash helmet is a worthy device but probably rarely instrumental in saving lives. Most people who get injured in automobile accidents, or are killed, suffer from a broken neck, broken back or have their chest crushed. The percentage of skull injuries in automobile accidents is relatively small. I think any good quality helmet which will protect the skull from penetration by sharp objects, such as a stone or a piece of the automobile, will give you reasonable protection.

For years I drove with a half-coverage helmet. Now I'm using a full-coverage and must confess I like it. It sits on the head more firmly than the other type did, though it has disadvantages too. From the point of giving you protection I don't think there's anything to choose between the two. As long as the helmet is of good quality and as long as it's fastened to your head so that it isn't going to blow off, it's going to do a good job for you.

What are your opinions on the choice between a glare shield and colored goggles or glasses?

I think that if I were racing anywhere except in America, I would wear a shield. In the first place, it doesn't lift up and in the second place, shields are generally much stronger than most goggles. The problem you face, with either form of protection, is the unusually large pebble which comes toward you like a missle. I have rarely seen them penetrate a glare shield, but they will frequently penetrate goggles and drive particles of glass into your eye.

However, there are other important considerations. Most of the U. S. courses on which we race are dusty. The shield gives you no protection against dust. Though I personally wear goggles, they continue to worry me because of the possibility of getting some of the glass stuck in an eyeball one of these days. Under some circumstances the glare shield would be better protection than the goggles; in others the goggles would be better. The goggles I do use have laminated safety glass in them but even at that they are a mental hazard.

The best are the type with a broad single lens which goes right across the eye area and fits in a soft foam rubber backing. The lens is usually replaceable heavy weight plastic.

For most people this is the ideal protection. Such goggles are nonmetallic so they can't be driven into the face. They are reasonably strong so as to absorb a certain amount of impact from a rock; and if the rock does penetrate and hit you in the eye, it won't drive particles of glass into the optic nerve.

What is your technique for getting a Cobra off the line in a hurry after the flag has dropped?

In competition I like to take the thing off the line with a bit of initial wheel spin which saves bothering about the clutch. I like to let the clutch in with enough speed to immediately break traction. I don't know whether this is the quickest technique, but I like it because it's easier on the driveline. You've got the clutch all the way home and the engine takes hold so that you have gas velocity through the carburetors up to the point where they are working properly. The engine is beginning to breathe, you can back off the throttle a little bit, let the tires take a grip and then charge.

With the car set up for racing, camshaft overlap is so great that if you let in the clutch at an idle and open the throttle, the engine will just stop. Gas velocity through the carburetors is so low the thing stalls out. The engine in the racing version doesn't really take hold until you've got about 5000 revs. I like to set the thing about 5000, drop the clutch on it, break traction on the back end and spin the wheels. Then back off the throttle, let the tires get a grip and charge off. This may cost a fraction of a second initially while you're sitting there burning a hole in the ground, but any other technique is going to cause a tremendous load on the clutch. Or you have to slip it like crazy to keep engine revs up while the car is standing still. You're going to lose a lot of time here while the carburetors are deciding how to work.

When do you make your first shift?

I like to shift at 6000 revs in long races. In short races, I run the thing up to 6500. If you get stuck and have to run 7000, it isn't going to hurt it. I like gearing in a long race to peak out about 6000 and in short races at about 6500. In almost any race, you run it up to your rev mark and shift.

Obviously you want to keep the engine turning just as fast as you possibly can. The longer you can keep that engine turning over at 6500 revs, the quicker you're going to go. At this speed it is developing maximum power. When engine speed falls off, power falls off faster.

When you're getting into the 100-mile-an hour range do you stay in fourth gear all the time or do you shift down occassionally?

Usually the gear ratios we're running in the Cobra gear box

will decide the absolute maximum speed and where you'll shift. The gear box we use at Nassau, for example, gives us about 130 miles an hour in third before we'd drop it into high gear. High gear will give us about 170. We spend a good deal of time in third.

How do you find the ideal line through a corner?

That depends on the car, the shape of the corner, type of surface, etc. There's really no such thing as one ideal line through any corner. The corner, car, driver, weather conditions, make and type of tire, tire pressure, shock absorber settings—all of these will combine to create an ideal line. All things being equal, you're bound to get variations depending on "set" of the car. All you can say is, that for this particular track this seems to be the most logical way to go through the corner.

There's two things to remember about cornering in competition. One is that the time you spend going in any other direction than straight ahead is time wasted. If you put the car completely sideways and broadside around the corner, you're very spectacular and impress spectators. But you're really not going very fast. The second thing is that the easiest way around any corner is keeping the car pointed the right way most of the time. This is the quick way. This is also the hard way because it is so difficult to get a car set up that will handle easily with a very small angle of drift.

It is much easier to design a car that will "set up" at 45 degrees to the line of flight. It handles beautifully with precision on dirt. Dirt-track cars have little suspension and very little in the way of a rigid chassis but when set up for drifting at 45 degrees to the line of flight, they handle beautifully. The really difficult thing is to get a car to go around the corner like it's "going on rails" which is the way to go. You'll probably be inside the corner to some extent—you're going to have a certain amount of drift—particularly in a car like the Cobra. This is also true of the Porsche Spyder. In that you have to drift through any sort of corner; a short, sharp corner and you have to broadside it—in a Maserati, also.

In some of the latest and most successful cars—the Formula I and some very late model, extremely exotic sports cars,—suspension is so good that you can't drift the car. You'll notice this if you're watching Formula I cars more than if you're watching only sports cars. Go to a track and watch Brabham in a Cooper and Clark in a Lotus. You'll see the tremendous difference in technique, in attitude of a car, between an ultra-modern Lotus chassis and the less exotic Cooper chassis. The difference of angles through a corner is something like 10 or 15 degrees between these two cars. Driven absolutely on the ragged edge, one car is still pointed down the track like it is on rails and the other is drifting at quite a large angle.

With a Cobra you've got to get some sort of angle on it. Whether you consider it a great deal of angle or a little bit, depends upon what you've been driving before. If you've been driving a Corvette, you'll think the Cobra runs in a straight line. If you've been driving a Formula Junior, you'll think that the Cobra hangs its tail out violently. It depends by what standards you judge it. We feel the Cobra hangs out more than a Ferrari, but a good deal less than Corvette's Sting Ray. *Ken, how do you bring the competition Cobra down to a reasonable speed before cornering?*

What you are doing is the same as for any other car under the same circumstances. It takes a bit of heavy brakes initially. This is essential so that you get the speed down to a point where when you engage third gear you aren't going to over-rev the engine. You want to come down into third gear, so you double clutch, go into third gear and at the same time maintain the braking. I make my change fairly deliberate and, at the same time, ease off the brakes and let them breathe a little.

If you're in a real hurry, you don't take it as easy, of course. You just stamp your foot on the brake pedal and hold it down with the ball of your foot, double clutch, while using the other half of your foot to work the throttle pedal, and come into the next lower gear. In a long race, we're usually not that critical over a fraction of a second in a lap. It's really more a question of stamina. I prefer to do the whole thing a little bit more

Cecil Bowman, Shelby American's engine tuner, prepares another Fairlane V8 for its test run in the modern dynomometer cell.

slowly and allow the brakes to breathe and let peak temperatures drop. Under the heavy braking we use at Sebring, you can stand on the corners and watch the brakes on these cars light up, with a dull red heat, like Roman candles, every time they slow to make a bend.

Again, heavy braking is used to get speed down to the point where it is safe to change down into second gear. More engines have burst going into a corner than anywhere else on the course. People shift at too high rev. They forget that it isn't the fact that the engine is being over-revved for any length of time that's important. It's the fact that it's being over-revved one fraction of a second. Over-revving an engine can do just as much damage in part of a second as in an hour. Because you spin the engine so fast stresses generated within the engine are greater than the capacity of the connecting rod's bolts to hold it. It doesn't matter if it's one second or a half second. If the bolts break, they're broke. That's all there is to it. There's no point in saying, "I only over-revved it for a second." You did the damage then.

Is there any situation where you'd use first gear during competition racing?

Very rarely. About the only place is one spot at Sebring where you use low gear once a lap on a ten-mile-an-hour corner. Shifting into low I use exactly the same technique. Its just a matter of going slower, and you can be a little more heavy footed about it.

Ken, if I read you right, what you're doing is making three separate braking operations. You let the car coast a bit—then you brake and shift—then it's brake and shift, coast, brake and shift. Is that right?

To some extent, yes. The coasting is only momentary. I'm only letting the brakes breathe from the time it takes me to get my foot from the brake pedal to the throttle pedal and back again in a leisurely manner, as I double clutch. It's probbaly a quarter second or something like that. Peak temperature gets so high on your brake discs that if you can get off the brakes even for an instant, the temperature collapses, which helps brake pad life. Of course, if you can't don't worry. Just press on regardless and hope that air scoops are putting enough air over the brakes to keep temperatures down.

On other occasions you will find a situation where you come to a low-speed corner at the end of a very high-speed straight. Here you may depend on brakes doing the entire job. You don't bother going through all the motions of down-shifting—just stand on the brakes, get the speed down to a point low enough and poke the thing straight into second gear, bypassing third altogether.

Then bypassing third and going into second is dandy if you can get away with it?

Yes, if you can get away with it. You know that by doing this you're losing some of the braking the engine will give you, so you're going to work the brakes that much harder. If you know the brakes will stand it, or if it's a short race or a race where you're only doing this once a lap, you can usually get away with it without losing your brakes. Just stand on them and let speed come right down to the point where you'll be able to use low gear. It's a technique which saves the amount of time it otherwise takes to change gears. Since maximum braking effort is determined by adhesion between tires and the ground, unless the car is set up very keenly, you're not going to gain very much advantage braking with the engine. We very often use this braking technique or, at least, I do.

Ken, we've talked a lot about heel and toe driving. What are your thoughts on this in regard to the Cobra?

It's perfectly feasible. I do it all the time, more out of force of habit than anything else—I've driven so many cars without synchromesh transmission. I was brought up on the cars that didn't have any low-end torque and am so used to maintaining engine speed at the exact point where the gear slides into engagement easily that I think I do it subconsciously.

I use the ball of my foot, under the big toe, on the brake pedal. Depending on the car, I can use my heel on the gas pedal or (what I usually find more convenient) rock my foot on the ball of the toe while using the side of my foot on the throttle pedal. You can do this without disturbing pressure on the brakes, especially if it is fairly high. My Ford wagon has an enormous servo on the brakes so that brake pressure is very little heavier than the throttle pressure. It's quite a trick to heel and toe on power brakes without locking up all of the wheels.

Do you mean to say that at the same time you're clutching, declutching and shifting the gears; you're also rocking your foot on the throttle off the brake?

Right. You'd use this technique for downshifting into a corner. You're going into a corner—braking to a critical point where you dare not take your foot off the brake but you want to be in a lower gear. Under these circumstances you will heel and toe to keep engine revolutions at the point where you can double clutch and get down to the next lower gear. When you let the clutch out, engine revs will already be matched up with revs of the rear axle so there's no sudden load placed on the rear wheels where it could cause the rear of the car to break away.

Would you suggest that a beginning driver practice this before racing?

Yes, in racing, this technique is absolutely essential. It is something you have to do. If you're driving anywhere close to the capabilities of the car, you can't afford to put any sudden torque loading on the rear wheels or you'll cause them to lose traction. If you do, and get away with it, you weren't going fast enough in the first place. Besides, you have to bear in mind that most racing cars are designed so that to get maximum braking you must depend on a certain amount of additional engine braking on rear wheels. Braking forces are calculated on your doing a series of things when you approach a corner at high speed. Brake hard to reduce your speed initially, go into a lower gear, and use brakes plus the engine loading to slow the car down. It is calculated that braking assistance from the engine will supplement braking ability of the rear brakes. In this way, all wheels come to a point of maximum retardation effort together. These are the circumstances under which you

Ken Miles leads a Ferrari through the entrance to the "pit straight" at Laguna Seca (near San Francisco) in June 1963. Cobras finished first, second and fourth in the event.

heel and toe. If you don't, then you lose just that fraction of a second which makes the difference between winning and losing a race.

Tell me, is the throttle pedal on your car in a special place so you can wiggle your foot better?

We set our racing cars up for individual drivers. For people with big feet, we leave a lot of room between the brake and throttle pedal so they can still reach over and hit it. A driver, like Dan Gurney, who is used to driving a properly set up machine may be extremely critical about pedal position. He'll say, "Well, I *want* them there." You know "this is it" and he gets them where he wants them. But the ultimate position for Dan Gurney is not necessarily the best position for someone else. We move them around to give the driver every advantage possible.

I have only moderate size feet so I can get down between a fairly narrow slot between the clutch pedal and the throttle pedal. I like the throttle pedal close to my foot so I can reach over there and use my heels on it. I don't like a big gap. I think a separation of about 1″ to 1½″ between the extreme edges of the two pedals is just about right.

How wide a brake pedal do you like?

As must as there's room for. In the Cobra, we have a rather narrow one. But a wide pedal puts that much less load on your feet. In a long race, particularly, your feet get tired.

What about throttle and brake action in getting out of a corner quickly?

Well, I've already braked heavily going into the corner with normal tires, wheels and brakes. After I've started turning the corner, I'm still braking, though already down to the gear I want to use through the corner. I usually like to have the car a bit sideways in the corner because then when I get off the brakes and get on the throttle, the car is already set and pointing the right way. I don't have to go through the motion of setting it up in the corner.

When you're going through a corner, all the tires are being pushed over in one direction. All the springs are moved over a little and the car is leaning over a bit. If you can come into the corner, or start the corner on the brakes, you've already set forces in motion to get the car into the proper attitude. Now, you're coming around the corner, on the brakes, with the car set at the proper attitude—the trick is to get off the brakes and catch it (the car) on the throttle without losing the "set" or without losing the drift angle. Then you have to take off from there on the throttle being careful not to give it too much or it'll bring the back end out. Too little will let it go straight ahead off the road on the outside of the corner.

Maintain a constant angle of slip through the corner until you get to the point where you start straightening out the steering wheel or getting the car pointed more down the track. As the car begins to see the straightaway, ease up on the angle of steering and start giving more and more power because the back wheels are now moving down the straight instead of moving off the track. This is especially important when exiting from a corner which leads onto a long straight which is almost a basic element of quick lap time. There's more time lost in the first 500 yards after a corner than anywhere else on a track.

Why is that?

Because this is the most critical point in the track. You see, if you are coming out of a corner at 90 miles an hour on a straightaway with a terminal velocity of 150 before you hit the end of the straight, you will have covered that distance in a specific amount of time. Now, if you come out of the same corner at 95 miles an hour, you will be that much faster all the way down. You can pass the man who came out at 90 miles an hour, even if he has the faster car.

This is why so many people say, "That car can't be stock. He pulled me down the straight." He didn't pull him down the straight, he just came out of the corner quicker. Because he came out of the corner faster he was still going faster at the other end of the straight. The thing people forget is that every mph gained coming out of a corner is a mile an hour you've gained the whole length of the straightaway. Most race courses consists in large part of straightaway, so this is where you make your time.

You said it is very important to get the car "set" into the proper attitude coming into a corner, and that the trick is to get off the brake and onto the throttle without destroying the set. Why is this so important?

If you lose the set, you've destroyed the whole system of forces set up. The easy way to handle any car is to come into the corner in a straight line on the brakes. Get off the brakes, open the throttle, establish cornering forces with the throttle. This is the simple way.

When doing this, by starting off on the brakes, you have a moment—a fraction of a second—where you're off the brakes and not yet on the throttle. The first set of forces you set up is collapsing and the second is not yet established. You must have the car in a condition where you can cope with these sudden changes. Supposing all the weight of the car is on the front wheels with your braking power, tires are leaning, suspension is leaning and the car is leaning over. All of a sudden, you get off the brake and what happens? You lose the weight transfer on the front wheels as the car rocks back. You're going to put on forward thrust instead of the previous rearward drag of the brakes. This is a critical point because you've collapsed one set of forces and you're going to replace them with another which is not going to give you the same general handling effect. Accordingly, you've got to make the change extremely quickly and with a very nice sense of balance. To catch the car—to change it from braking attitude to an accelerating attitude—is extremely tricky.

What will happen if you don't catch it?

One of two things. When you make a transition from brake to throttle, and give the car too much throttle you will either generate gross oversteer because you've lost traction on the back, or understeer because the torque dividing differential will lock up and pull you straight off the course. Either could happen very easily.

Or you'll find that between getting off the brakes and getting on the throttle, the car has straightened up and started to go forward. You can't get it all set again, so, instead of making a nice smooth curve when you turn, you make a jog in the middle of the corner. Since the corner went around anyway, you've lost that much road and time. Instead of being on the inside of the turn, you may have moved out and are drifting towards the outside. There's only one fast line around this corner for your particular car. If you deviate from that line by only a foot, you're going to go around the corner slower. You've got to keep this system established—keep the car facing the right way so you're on the right line. This is extremely difficult to do.

How do you come off of the brake and onto the throttle?

It depends on the circumstances. You can do this—and I've done it this way: Have only half your foot on the brake and be gradually giving it more throttle with the right half of your foot while you're getting off the brake with the left. You're going to change the established forces anyway and the thing to do is to get changed as quickly and as smoothly as possible.

Ken, what general advice would you, as a very skilled and knowledgeable driver, give to the buyer of a Cobra?

I can give him that general advice in two very short words: "Drive carefully!"